RAND NATIONAL SECURITY RESEARCH DIVISION

Iran's Influence in Afghanistan

Implications for the U.S. Drawdown

Alireza Nader, Ali G. Scotten, Ahmad Idrees Rahmani, Robert Stewart, Leila Mahnad

This research was sponsored by a private foundation and was conducted within the International Security and Defense Policy Center of the RAND National Security Research Division (NSRD). NSRD conducts research and analysis on defense and national security topics for the U.S. and allied defense, foreign policy, homeland security, and intelligence communities and foundations and other nongovernmental organizations that support defense and national security analysis.

Library of Congress Cataloging-in-Publication Data

ISBN: 978-0-8330-8592-4

The RAND Corporation is a nonprofit institution that helps improve policy and decisionmaking through research and analysis. RAND's publications do not necessarily reflect the opinions of its research clients and sponsors.

Support RAND—make a tax-deductible charitable contribution at www.rand.org/giving/contribute.html

RAND® is a registered trademark.

Cover image by AP Photo/Ebrahim Noroozi

RAND OFFICES
SANTA MONICA, CA • WASHINGTON, DC
PITTSBURGH, PA • NEW ORLEANS, LA • JACKSON, MS • BOSTON, MA
CAMBRIDGE, UK • BRUSSELS, BE
www.rand.org

Preface

The U.S. drawdown from Afghanistan may lead to greater instability and a vacuum in that country. The Islamic Republic of Iran, one the most powerful regional actors in Afghanistan, is poised to exercise substantial influence there after the U.S. drawdown. In addition, the drawdown may provide Iran with the opportunity to strengthen ties with other powers involved in Afghanistan, such as India and Russia. Greater Iranian influence in Afghanistan could help Iran alleviate economic and political pressures resulting from its nuclear dispute.

At the same time, the election of Hassan Rouhani as Iran's president may provide a new opportunity for greater U.S.-Iran cooperation in Afghanistan, as was the case after the Taliban's overthrow in 2001. Both countries have convergent interests in Afghanistan, including the prevention of Taliban rule. Such potential cooperation will depend on the status of nuclear negotiations between Iran and the United States, and the state of overall tensions between the two nations.

This study examines Iran's historical interests in Afghanistan and its current policies in that country. The study pays particular attention to key aspects of the Iranian-Afghan relationship, including Iran's cultural, political, economic, and ideological ties to Afghanistan. The study explores the extent and limits of Iranian influence in Afghanistan, including Tehran's relations with key Afghan groups and constituencies.

Furthermore, the study analyzes Iran's relations with regional powers, such as India, Russia, and Pakistan, in light of the U.S. drawdown. Finally, the study explores the implications of Iranian influence for the United States as it withdraws most of its combat forces from Afghanistan.

This research was sponsored by a private foundation and was conducted within the International Security and Defense Policy Center of the RAND National Security Research Division (NSRD). NSRD conducts research and analysis on defense and national security topics for the U.S. and allied defense, foreign policy, homeland security, and intelligence communities and foundations and other nongovernmental organizations that support defense and national security analysis.

For more information on the International Security and Defense Policy Center, see http://www.rand.org/nsrd/ndri/centers/isdp.html or contact the director (contact information is provided on the web page).

Contents

Summary

This report examines Iran's cultural, political, and economic influence in Afghanistan, especially in light of the U.S. drawdown. Many American policymakers and analysts worry that the departure of most international military forces from Afghanistan may result in greater instability there, which can be exploited by foreign powers, such as the Islamic Republic of Iran.

A state of rivalry between Iran and the United States, exacerbated by tensions over Iran's nuclear program, has often meant competition in other areas, including Afghanistan. Tehran has viewed the decadelong U.S. presence in Afghanistan with anxiety. Iran's fears of U.S. military strikes against its nuclear facilities, or perceived American plans to overthrow the Iranian regime, may have motivated it to provide measured military support to Afghan insurgents battling U.S. forces and the International Security Assistance Force (ISAF). Iran also actively opposes the Bilateral Security Agreement (BSA) being negotiated between Afghanistan and the United States.

U.S. policymakers may naturally think that Iran will seek to exploit the drawdown and undermine American interests in Afghanistan. However, the departure of U.S. forces from Afghanistan, a new pragmatic government in Tehran, and a possible resolution to the nuclear crisis may provide greater cooperation between Tehran and Washington in Afghanistan.

Iranian objectives in Afghanistan align with most U.S. interests. Therefore, Iranian influence in Afghanistan following the drawdown of international forces need not necessarily be a cause of concern for the United States. Much like the United States, Iran wants to see a stable Afghanistan with a government free of Taliban control, and Iran seeks to stem the tide of Sunni extremism in the region.

The extent to which Iran would be willing to directly cooperate with the United States in Afghanistan largely depends on the status of the Iranian nuclear dispute. It is important to note, however, that even if U.S.-Iran tensions remain, Iran's activities in Afghanistan are unlikely to run counter to the overall objectives of the United States.

The United States should attempt to cooperate with Iran in countering narcotics in Afghanistan and encourage efforts to bring Tehran and Kabul to an agreement over water sharing. Because the Taliban insurgency is largely funded through drug trafficking, counternarcotics efforts would contribute to Afghanistan's security. Tensions over scarce water resources could also fuel instability if left unaddressed.

While many of the disagreements between the two countries appear intractable and beholden to political interests in Tehran and Washington, combating drug trafficking and addressing water-usage issues would be relatively uncontroversial and nonpolitical. It could also lead to increased mutual trust that would benefit broader U.S.-Iran relations. To this end, the United States could lend logistical or financial support to the UN-facilitated Triangular Initiative, which fosters coordination among Iran, Pakistan, and Afghanistan in countering the drug trade. With regards to the Iran-Afghan water dispute, the United States should become active—through the UN and development organizations—in facilitating a mutually agreed upon water-usage system.

Iran is hedging its bets in order to be prepared for a variety of outcomes following the U.S. drawdown. Iran has maintained close ties with Afghanistan's Tajik and Hazara populations in order to gain political influence and protect its interests after the U.S. drawdown.

On the other hand, Iran appears to be open to engaging with the Taliban after the U.S. drawdown. The extent of engagement will depend on the Taliban's posture toward Iran and its treatment of the Afghan Shia.

Iran will continue attempting to build soft influence in Afghanistan, especially in the realms of education and the media. Iran has been building and buttressing pro-Iranian schools, mosques, and media centers. Much of this activity centers on western and northern Afghanistan, in addition to Kabul. Afghan schools have received thousands of Iranian books, many of which espouse the values of the Islamic republic.

However, Iran will face challenges in winning over the Afghan populace. The Pashtuns, who are more closely affiliated with Pakistan, remain wary of the Iranians. Meanwhile, many of the Shia Hazara do not favor Iran's system of governance. In recent years, Hazara political parties have made efforts not to be seen simply as Iranian proxies, and are likely to seek support from Western countries as well.

Although set to remain generally positive, Iran-Afghan relations likely will experience strain over water disputes and the issue of refugees. Exacerbated by drought, water-sharing disputes are likely to persist as a significant sticking point between Tehran and Kabul as Afghanistan's plan to boost its agricultural sector will lead to increased water usage upstream, affecting Iran's supplies. Both countries suffer from a shortage of water, with Iran's eastern provinces bordering Afghanistan being particularly water challenged.

In recent years, the status of Afghan refugees in Iran has become a highly politicized issue. Iran has more Afghan refugees than any other country after Pakistan. As economic conditions in Iran have deteriorated, Afghan refugees have come to be seen by many as a burden and have been subjected to discrimination and abuse at the hands of the Iranian government. Numerous protests have erupted in Afghanistan over Iran's treatment of refugees. Furthermore, Iran has attempted to use the threat of mass deportation of Afghans as a means of pressuring the Kabul government to adopt policies favorable to the Islamic Republic.

Following the withdrawal of U.S. forces and ISAF from Afghanistan in 2016, Iranian and U.S. strategy there will be influenced in large part by the actions of Pakistan, India, and Russia. As the world's only superpower, the United States will continue to play an important role in Afghanistan following the ISAF drawdown. It is important, however, to bear in mind that U.S. influence there will be determined in large part by its relations with regional actors and, in turn, their relations with one another. Iran's overall interests in Afghanistan align with the core U.S., Indian, and Russian objectives in Afghanistan: to prevent the country from again becoming dominated by the Taliban and a safe haven for al Qaeda. Therefore, Iranian cooperation with regional actors in Afghanistan could serve U.S. interests.

In the event of a nuclear deal, it is prudent that the United States directly engage Iran in bilateral discussions regarding Afghanistan and pursue joint activities that would serve their mutual interests and build much-needed trust.

Acknowledgments

The authors would like to thank Gary Sick and Paul Miller for their helpful reviews.

Abbreviations

ANSF	Afghan National Security Forces
BSA	Bilateral Security Agreement
CENTO	Central Treaty Organization
IAEA	International Atomic Energy Agency
IPI	Iran-Pakistan-India [pipeline]
ISAF	International Security Assistance Force
LNG	liquefied natural gas
NATO	North Atlantic Treaty Organization
NSRD	RAND National Security Research Division
RPG	rifle-propelled grenade
SCO	Shanghai Cooperation Organisation
TAPI	Turkmenistan-Afghanistan-Pakistan-India pipeline

CHAPTER ONE

Introduction

This study explores Iranian influence in Afghanistan and the implications for the United States after the departure of most American forces from Afghanistan. Iran has substantial economic, political, cultural, and religious leverage in Afghanistan. There is a chance that Tehran can use its influence to undermine U.S. interests, especially if a failure to resolve the Iranian nuclear crisis leads to increasing tensions between the United States and Iran, including a possible military conflict.

However, the election of Hassan Rouhani as Iran's president and a potential breakthrough in nuclear negotiations could herald greater cooperation between Iran and the United States in Afghanistan. Both Iran and the United States share an interest in thwarting the Taliban's victory and ensuring a more stable Afghanistan.

Afghanistan faces an uncertain future after the U.S. drawdown in 2016. Kabul is also likely to receive continued economic and financial support from Washington, including payments to the Afghan armed forces and the national police.

But Afghanistan's stability is far from certain. Kabul faces an obdurate insurgency that is likely to exploit the U.S. and international drawdown. The Afghan government will also face many economic difficulties in future years. Afghanistan is highly dependent on international economic aid, and many Afghan businesses profit from U.S. and International Security Assistance Force (ISAF) military activities. Although endowed with great natural and mineral wealth, Afghanistan has a negligible industrial base. Its exports of fruits, nuts, carpets, and semiprecious stones are not substantial.[1] It appears that the illicit economy in Afghanistan—especially opium production—is a bigger source of revenue than most (if not all) other economic sectors.[2]

There is cause to be worried about Afghanistan's future economic stability. The 1992 overthrow and subsequent murder of Mohammad Najibullah, Afghanistan's Soviet-backed ruler, is often attributed to Moscow's decision to cease financial support to his government as the Soviet Union began to unravel.[3] Najibullah had managed to survive the Soviet troop withdrawal in 1989 and hold off the Afghan Mujahideen.[4] But he could only do so with substantial

---

[1] Victor Mallet, "Afghanistan's Forgotten Crisis: Its Economy," *Financial Times*, May 20, 2013.

[2] Michael Nicoletti, "Opium Production and Distribution: Poppies, Profits and Power in Afghanistan," thesis, DePaul University, 2011.

[3] Afghan researcher, interview with the authors, January 4, 2013.
   The authors conducted fieldwork in Afghanistan by interviewing Afghan researchers, analysts, political leaders, and former government officials. All interviews took place throughout Afghanistan and were translated by the authors.

[4] World Bank, *Afghanistan in Transition: Looking Beyond 2014*, Vol. 1, Washington, D.C.: World Bank, May 2012.

Soviet aid. Although circumstances are different now, one can argue that the Afghan central government is similarly dependent on American and international support. The Western military drawdown from Afghanistan could weaken the Afghan economy, and ultimately Kabul's ability to hold off the Taliban. Afghanistan's ability to build a more independent economy will also play a major role in preserving political stability. The economic role of neighboring countries, especially Pakistan and Iran, is important in this regard.

However, the biggest problem facing Afghanistan may be political corruption. The Afghan government is often accused of nepotism, and it is far from certain that Hamid Karzai and his supporters will completely relinquish power after the 2014 presidential election.[5] Technically, Karzai cannot run again, but there are indications that he is planning to shape the next government according to his own personal interests. Many Afghans, including those interviewed by RAND, are highly concerned about the possibility of corrupt and nondemocratic elections.[6] According to a survey conducted by the Asia Foundation in 2011, Afghans consider corruption to be the third-biggest problem their country faces, after insecurity and unemployment.[7]

Another major problem faced by Afghanistan is the lack of ethnic and religious unity.[8] The Afghan government, although led by Karzai, a Pashtun, is heavily dominated by the Tajik, and to a lesser extent the Hazara. Whoever succeeds Karzai as president will have to possess the ability to bridge the gap between Afghanistan's rival ethnic and minority groups. This may prove to be more difficult in the absence of substantial U.S. and ISAF military forces. The Afghan National Security Forces (ANSF) have received extensive training and funding from the United States and its partners. The United States alone has invested approximately $50 billion since 2002 in developing the ANSF.[9]

Yet the ANSF is riven by persistent challenges, including ethno-religious divisions and attrition. A report released in April 2011 states that although the overall composition of the Afghan National Army reflects the ethnic makeup of Afghanistan, and while approximately 40 percent of the ANSF are ethnically Pashtun, only 3 percent of soldiers are southern Pashtuns, which has significant implications for the army's credibility.[10] Furthermore, areas with Pashtun-majority inhabitants, such as southern Afghanistan, are patrolled by non-Pashtuns, raising the specter of increased violence after the drawdown.

Neighboring powers, such as Pakistan and Iran, tend to favor certain ethnic and religious minorities over others, potentially exacerbating Afghanistan's ethno-religious divisions. Pakistan is known to have strong ties to the Pashtun, while Iran favors the Tajik and Hazara. India also has closer ties to the Tajik, especially given its history of supporting the anti-Taliban Northern Alliance. Of course, the picture in Afghanistan is not completely black and white. Pakistan does have ties to non-Pashtun groups, while Iran and India have tried to cultivate

---

[5] Jessica Donati, "Afghan President Karzai's Brother to Offer Him Role If Elected," Reuters, October 11, 2013.

[6] Former senior Afghan government official, interview with the authors, February 24, 2013.

[7] Yama Torabi, *The Growing Challenge of Corruption in Afghanistan: Reflections on a Survey of the Afghan People, Part 3 of 4*, Washington, D.C.: Asia Foundation, 2012.

[8] Senior Afghan security official, interview with the authors, February 19, 2013.

[9] "Report: Afghans Paid $3.9 Billion in Bribes Last Year," Afghanistan Study Group, February 11, 2013.

[10] Sven Mikser, *Transition in Afghanistan: Assessing the Security Effort*, NATO Parliamentary Assembly, draft general report, April 8, 2011.

relations with Pashtun groups, including the Taliban. But the drawdown has the potential to widen Afghanistan's divisions and invite greater neighboring support for rival Afghan groups.

Iran, in particular, could strengthen relations with the anti-Taliban forces it supported prior to 2001. And it is not inconceivable that Iran, India, and Russia could reestablish their previous partnership in support of a new Northern Alliance battling the Pashtun-dominated and Pakistan-supported insurgency. According to one influential Afghan official, "the old coalition of India, Russia, and Iran might rise again."[11] This could portend not only more violence in Afghanistan but also the sort of civil war not seen since the 1990s, when various Mujahideen groups fought each other for control of the country.[12]

Although Afghan cities tend to be more stable, future instability in Afghanistan could be strongly felt in rural areas that are beyond central authority. International economic and security assistance has not penetrated rural areas as fully as urban areas, making them more susceptible to violence after the drawdown.[13] According to a former Afghan official interviewed by RAND, "the development of the country since 2001 has never reached the village."[14] This view has been corroborated by research conducted by the Asia Foundation.[15] Rural areas continue to exist in conditions similar to those during and before Taliban rule.[16] In the absence of a large number of Western troops, the Taliban will attempt to make gains in much of Afghanistan. And Pakistan could seek to exploit this for its own benefit.

Iran has several major interests in Afghanistan that it wants to protect, but while Tehran supports a stable Afghan central government, it does not necessarily want a strong Afghanistan that can challenge its interests. Nor does Tehran want powers such as Pakistan to gain influence in the region at its expense.

At the same time, Iran does not want a chaotic Afghanistan, or one ruled by the Taliban. So while the U.S. drawdown provides certain opportunities for Iran, it is not a zero-sum game for the Iranian government. An Afghan analyst we interviewed put it succinctly: "The Iranians are smarter than to ask all the Americans to leave, because they know that if all the American troops pull out, then Afghanistan will completely fall under the control of Pakistan."[17]

While Iran will seek to increase its power in Afghanistan, its overall interests will likely converge with American priorities. This does not mean that Iran will necessarily join the Western coalition in Afghanistan, or that it will become a partner with the United States. There may be a sense of competition between the two over Afghanistan. But both Tehran and Washington could pursue their respective interests in ways that are mutually beneficial. Iran's influence in Afghanistan is not limitless, and it is unlikely to dominate its neighbor once the United States leaves. This provides an opportunity for cooperation rather than zero-sum competition.

---

[11] Afghan official, interview with the authors, February 21, 2013.

[12] Zalmay Khalizad, "Afghanistan in 1994: Civil War and Destruction," *Asian Survey*, Vol. 35, No. 2, February 1995, p. 147.

[13] Siegfried O. Wolf, "Post-2014 Afghanistan: Future Scenarios from Structure and Agency Perspectives," *Journal of South Asian Development*, Vol. 8, No. 2, 2013.

[14] Former Afghan official, interview with the authors, January 2, 2013.

[15] Abdul-Qayum Mohmand, *The Prospects for Economic Development in Afghanistan: Reflections on a Survey of the Afghan People*, Part 2 of 4, Washington, D.C.: Asia Foundation, 2012.

[16] Senior Afghan security official, interview with the authors, January 2, 2013.

[17] Afghan analyst, interview with the authors, January 4, 2013.

This study examines Iran's historical interests in Afghanistan and its current policies in that country, and explores the potential implications for U.S. policy. The research is based on field interviews in Afghanistan, the use of primary sources in Dari and Persian, and scholarly research in English. Chapter Two explores Afghanistan's current situation and its substantial but complicated cultural, religious, political, and economic ties with Iran. Chapter Three examines Iran's relations with other regional actors in Afghanistan, including Pakistan, India, and Russia. Chapter Four assesses implications for U.S. interests.

Iran and Afghanistan: A Complicated Relationship

Iran's ambitions in Afghanistan should not be viewed as hegemonic. Tehran does not believe that it can completely dominate its neighbor; instead, it has certain interests to protect, including securing its eastern border, preserving the flow of water from Afghanistan, countering narcotics, and dealing with the large Afghan refugee population on its soil. Tehran is particularly anxious to prevent a total Taliban victory in Afghanistan and the expansion of Pakistani power. It also does not desire a long-term U.S. military presence in Afghanistan; Iran is the only regional power that has actively opposed the Bilateral Security Agreement (BSA) being negotiated between Kabul and Washington.

The Iranian government has attempted to achieve its objectives through a variety of means. Iran's cultural and religious bonds allow it to exercise influence over key ethnic and religious groups, including the Tajik and Hazara, and their respective political parties. Iran is also an important economic partner; it has provided Afghanistan with up to US$500 million in development aid and is one of Afghanistan's major trading partners. Moreover, Iran maintains close ties to various militias and armed groups both allied with and battling U.S. forces.

Iran and Afghanistan have much in common: a shared language, deep historical and cultural bonds, and at times common enemies. The security and stability of one is dependent on the other. But it would be wrong to assume that their relationship is trouble free. While some Afghans view Iran as a warm neighbor, and a possible protector, many resent what they perceive to be Tehran's heavy-handed interference in their affairs.

Many Afghans—especially the Tajiks, Hazara, and other non-Pashtuns—are particularly worried about Pakistan and its ally, the Taliban. And while the Taliban is a Pashtun-dominated political movement, many Afghans, including the Pashtun, are worried about Pakistani influence in Afghanistan's internal affairs. It is thus tempting for Iran to view itself as a natural counterweight to Pakistan, and the protector of Afghanistan's embattled minorities. After all, Tehran supported Tajik and Shia (Hazara) Mujahideen commanders during the Soviet occupation of Afghanistan, and later provided aid to the Northern Alliance against the Taliban.[1]

Close but Not Exclusive Ties with the Afghan Tajik and Shia

The cultural and religious ties between Iran and Afghanistan are strong, and can provide Tehran with a substantial amount of political leverage. According to a prominent Afghan

---

[1] Mohsen M. Milani, "Iran's Policy Towards Afghanistan," *Middle East Journal*, Vol. 60, No. 2, Spring 2006.

Shia leader, "Iran currently has a strong presence in Afghanistan but most of it is unofficial. It all goes back to culture, customs, and language."[2] Dari, one of Afghanistan's two official languages, spoken by roughly 50 percent of the population, is closely related to Persian (Farsi), Iran's official language.[3] Most Iranians and Afghans would probably be able to communicate with each other, depending on local dialects and accents. Moreover, millions of other Afghans, including many members of the educated elite, have lived and studied in Iran and are very familiar with the Persian language. Afghanistan's Dari-speaking Tajiks in particular may feel a cultural affinity with Iran. Much of western and northeastern Afghanistan, in addition to major cities like Kabul, is populated by Tajiks.[4]

Most Afghans, including Tajiks, are Sunni Muslims, whereas Iran's population is between 90 and 95 percent Shia.[5] Nevertheless, a significant portion of Afghanistan's population, perhaps nearly 20 percent, belongs to the Shia sect.[6] Among them are the Hazara, a much-persecuted minority group of Asiatic origin inhabiting what is known as the Hazarajat, a region in Bamyan and surrounding provinces.[7] The Hazara are the largest Shia community in Afghanistan, although there are other Shia groups, such as the Qizilbash, the Farsiwan, and the Sayyeds.

The Hazara, who have traditionally looked to Tehran for religious and political guidance, have emerged as important social and political actors in Afghanistan since the 2001 overthrow of the Taliban. Hazara politicians occupy important government posts in Kabul, and are likely to retain them after the U.S. drawdown. Karim Khalili, the Afghan vice president and leader of the Hazara Hezb-e Wahdat-e Islami, is likely to play an important role in the post-2014 government. The Hazara, who suffered heavy discrimination at the hands of the Taliban, have also become more explicit in the expression of their Shia faith. Public processions marking Shia holy days, once forbidden under the Taliban, have become much more common on the streets of Kabul and other cities.[8]

Many of the Hazara and other Afghan Shia sympathize with Iran, much more so than with Pakistan, for example. One Afghan Shia leader stated: "Looking at the past, we can see that Iran hasn't really played any role in insecurity or destabilization of Afghanistan. On the other hand, you can see that Pakistan is not willing to have a stable Afghanistan by its side. From the time of Jihad until now, Pakistan has played ninety percent of the role in destroying the infrastructures of Afghanistan."[9]

---

[2] Prominent Afghan Shia leader, interview with the authors, January 1, 2013.

[3] According to the Afghanistan section of the CIA's World Factbook, the Turkic languages spoken in Afghanistan, including Uzbek and Turkmen, are considered the third official languages in the areas where the majority speaks them. See www.cia.gov/library/publications/the-world-factbook/geos/af.html.

[4] Nassim Jawad, *Afghanistan: A Nation of Minorities*, London: Minority Rights Group, 1992.

[5] Saied Reza Ameli and Hamideh Molaei, "Religious Affiliation and Intercultural Sensitivity: Interculturality Between Shia and Sunni Muslims in Iran," *International Journal of Intercultural Relations*, Vol. 36, No. 1, 2012.

[6] *The World Factbook*, Afghanistan.

[7] Niamatullah Ibrahimi, "The Dissipation of Political Capital Among Afghanistan's Hazaras: 2001–2009," working paper no. 51, Crisis States Research Center, London School of Economics and Political Science, June 2009.

[8] "Roshd-e Tashi'o dar Afghanistan va Naghsh-e Iran" ["The Growth of Shi'ism in Afghanistan and the Role of Iran"], BBC Persian, January 6, 2009.

[9] Prominent Afghan Shia leader, interview with the authors, January 1, 2013.

Iran is likely to use its ties with the Hazara (and other Shia) to exercise influence in Afghanistan. According to one source, up to 55 members of the parliament are Shia and may have connections to Iran.[10] Many Afghan Shia leaders also feel a personal religious affinity with Iran.[11]

Nevertheless, the Iranian government has also courted Pashtun groups, including the Taliban. Iran has long maintained a relationship with Gulbeddin Hekmatyar's Pashtun-dominated Hezb-e Islami. Hekmatyar sought refuge in Iran from 1996, when the Taliban took over Kabul, until 2002, when Iran expelled Hekmatyar from the country.[12] And it is likely that he has received some amount of Iranian support in his battle against U.S. forces and ISAF in the past decade.[13] An influential Afghan told us that Afghanistan's "ex-ambassador to Iran was also a previous member of Hezb-e Islami and was so close to the Islamic Republic that we all know about the bags of money that he was receiving."[14]

The Iranian government has also engaged in political discussions with Taliban representatives. Moreover, Taliban delegations have visited Tehran as part of Iranian-sponsored peace talks.[15] Although Iran views the Tajik and Hazara as being its best interlocutors in Afghanistan, it nevertheless views the Pashtun and even the Taliban as important to its overall strategy.

There may be a recognition among some elements in Iran that today's Taliban, although not friendly toward Iranian interests, is nevertheless not the zealous and fanatic Taliban of the 1990s.[16] If anything, the Taliban and the Islamic Republic share a common foe, the United States. Tehran may realize that the Taliban is likely to be a major factor in Afghanistan after the U.S. drawdown. Therefore, it makes sense that Iran is hedging its bets and not entirely relying on its traditional Shia and Tajik partners. As one influential Afghan told us, Iran is "confident of the conditions to an extent. Even if the Taliban comes to power, Iran has a way to deal with the Taliban."[17]

The Islamic Republic, although wary of the Taliban, has not allowed religious and ideological issues to interfere with political expediency. Tehran has historically worked with non-Shia groups throughout the Middle East and Muslim world; although Iran maintains close ties to Shia and related groups, such as the Lebanese Hezbollah (and the Allawite regime in Syria), it nevertheless does not use sect as a decisive factor in its political calculations.

---

[10] Ibid.

[11] "Rahbar Shi'ayan-e Afghanistan: Iran Olguye Monasebi baraye Keshvar haye Islami ast" ["Afghanistan's Shi'a Leader: Iran Is an Appropriate Role Model for Islamic Countries"], Iranian Students' News Agency, November 22, 2010; "Majara-ye Didar-e Marja'e Shi'iyan-e Afghanistan ba Rahbar-e Enghelab" ["Afghanistan's Shia Marja Visits the Leader of the Revolution"], Shia-Online, May 6, 2013.

[12] "Iran 'Expels' Afghan Warlord," BBC News, February 26, 2002.

[13] Influential Afghan, interview with the authors, February 23, 2013.

[14] Ibid.

[15] Emma Graham-Harrison, "Afghan Taliban Send Delegation to Iran," *The Guardian*, June 3, 2013; "Taliban Confirms FNA Report on Recent Visit to Tehran," Fars News Agency, June 3, 2013; Chris Zambelis, "The Day After: Iran's Quiet Taliban Diplomacy Reflects Preparations for a Post-U.S. Afghanistan," *Terrorism Monitor*, Vol. 11, No. 21, 2013.

[16] Mohsen Milani, "Iran's Ties to the Taliban," *The Iran Primer*, United States Institute of Peace, August 10, 2011.

[17] Afghan media leader, interview with the authors, February 23, 2013.

Iran's Political Role in Afghanistan

Iran viewed Afghanistan as important to its national security even before its 1979 revolution. Iran's last monarch, Mohammad Reza Pahlavi, worried about the spread of communism in Afghanistan and provided economic and military support to various Afghan parties. The Islamic Republic, which replaced the Iranian monarchy, shared similar concerns.

Iran's revolutionary leader, Ayatollah Ruhollah Khomeini, was opposed to Soviet domination of Afghanistan and was a proponent of the spread of the Islamic Revolution under *velayat-e faghih* (rule of the supreme jurisprudent).[18] The Shia ulema of Afghanistan at the time espoused a range of views on the role of religion in government, and Tehran provided the most support to the groups that followed Khomeini's line. Several Afghan Shia groups based out of Iran developed into Afghanistan's Hazara-dominated Hezb-e Wahdat political party.[19]

However, the Islamic Republic, distracted by internal unrest and Saddam Hussein's 1980 invasion, was not able to devote much attention or resources to its eastern neighbor. The Afghan Mujahideen, dominated by Sunni groups, received more support from Pakistan, Saudi Arabia, and the United States, although Iran did help organize and direct Afghan Shia Mujahideen forces.[20]

Iran's involvement in Afghanistan increased after the Soviet departure and the fall of the Najibullah government in 1992.[21] The war with Iraq ended in 1988, allowing a more stable Iran to spend resources to spread its influence in Afghanistan.[22] From 1992 to 1996, Tehran backed several Mujahideen groups fighting for control of Afghanistan, particularly Kabul. Iran not only supported the Burhanuddin Rabbani government in Kabul at the time but was also simultaneously providing assistance to Hezb-e Wahdat, which was occasionally engaged in armed struggle with the central government, thus demonstrating Iran's flexible approach to Afghanistan.[23] After the Taliban's relatively rapid victory in 1996, Iran backed what came to be known as the Northern Alliance (or Northern Front): an Afghan opposition movement composed of militias centered on Tajik, Uzbek, and Hazara strongmen from northern Afghanistan.

Iran's relations with Taliban-ruled Afghanistan were often tense, if not outright hostile. The Taliban, heavily influenced by Wahhabi religious doctrine emanating from Saudi Arabia, viewed Shia-dominated Iran as a heresy.[24] The Taliban's persecution of Afghan Shia, particularly the Hazara, further complicated relations between Tehran and Kabul.

---

[18]   Alvin Z. Rubinstein, "The Soviet Union and Iran Under Khomeini," *International Affairs*, Vol. 57, No. 4, Autumn 1981, p. 599.

[19]   Vahid Mojde, *Ravabat-e Siyasi-ye Iran va Afghanistan dar Qarn-e Bistom* [*Iran and Afghanistan's Political Relations in the 20th Century*], Maiwand, Afghanistan: Maiwand Publishing Company, 2010; Niamatullah Ibrahimi, "The Failure of a Clerical Proto-State: Hazarajat, 1979–1984," working paper no. 6, Crisis States Research Centre, London School of Economics and Political Science, September 2006.

[20]   Crises Analysis Group Pakistan's Strategic Studies Center, "Bohran-e Afghanistan az chand Didgah" ["The Afghanistan Crisis from Various Viewpoints"], *Strategic Studies*, Vol. 11, No. 3, 1988.

[21]   Mojde, 2010.

[22]   Milani, 2006.

[23]   Mojde, 2010.

[24]   William Maley, *The Foreign Policy of the Taliban*, New York: Council on Foreign Relations Press, February 2000.

The Islamic Republic views itself as a protector of the Shia "downtrodden," and felt particularly chagrined at the Taliban's oppression of the Hazara.[25] The Taliban's August 1998 massacre of the Hazara and murder of Iranian diplomats in Mazar-e Sharif brought relations to a new low. In response to the murders and other provocations, Iran amassed tens of thousands of troops along its border with Afghanistan.[26] It appeared that the Islamic Republic was poised for an invasion of its eastern neighbor.

Iran and the Taliban never came to direct blows. But Tehran may have been more convinced than ever before that the Northern Alliance was its best bet. Along with Russia and India, the Islamic Republic became one of the main supporters of the anti-Taliban movement.

All three countries were unified in the belief that a fundamentalist Sunni Islamic government in the region would have a negative impact on regional security and stability, limiting trade and investment in the newly independent Central Asian states.

The 2001 U.S. invasion of Afghanistan provided Iran with an opportunity to expand its influence in Afghanistan. The swift overthrow of the Taliban by American and Northern Alliance forces rid Tehran of an implacable foe. With American support, the Northern Alliance and its allies assumed power in Kabul. However, the ethnic and religious makeup of Afghanistan presented problems. The Northern Alliance was dominated by Dari-speaking Tajiks, whereas an estimated 40 percent of Afghanistan's population is Pashtun.[27] Hamid Karzai, a polished and urbane Pashtun from a prominent Afghan clan, emerged as the leading candidate to become the country's new leader. However, the Northern Alliance leadership, keen to promote its own ethnic and religious interests on the new government, was resistant to a Pashtun president.

Iran played a crucial role in persuading the Northern Alliance to support Karzai. According to Ambassador James Dobbins, the American envoy to Afghanistan at the time (and the current American envoy to Afghanistan), it was the Iranian envoy, Mohammad Javad Zarif, who convinced Younis Qanooni, a powerful Northern Alliance leader, to back Karzai. Dobbins also received an offer from an Iranian general to assist in training the Afghan National Army.[28] According to a prominent Afghan leader, "If it weren't for Iran, our Western friends would not be able to come today so easily and tell us about all the things they have done for us."[29]

Iran's support for U.S. interests in Afghanistan was surprising given the level of mutual hostility between Tehran and Washington. The major reason for Iran's behavior was sheer pragmatism. The U.S. overthrow of the Taliban benefited Iranian interests. But there were other reasons for Iran's helpful policies.

Iranian President Mohammad Khatami had adopted a policy of engagement with the West. A proponent of "dialogue among civilizations," Khatami was eager to decrease tensions not only with regional powers such as Saudi Arabia but also with European countries and the

---

[25] Dexter Filkins, "Afghans Report Ethnic Massacre by Taliban," *Los Angeles Times*, September 18, 1998.

[26] Douglas Jehl, "Iran Holds Taliban Responsible for 9 Diplomats' Deaths," *The New York Times*, September 11, 1998.

[27] Jawad, 1992.

[28] Jim Dobbins, "Engaging Iran," *The Iran Primer*, United States Institute of Peace, October 22, 2013.

[29] Afghan religious leader, interview with the authors, January 1, 2013.

United States.[30] Instead of exporting the Islamic revolution to the wider Middle East, Khatami wanted to build cooperative relations with neighboring countries and global powers.

To understand Iran's involvement in Afghanistan, one has to understand its relations with the United States. Iran's engagement with the United States in Afghanistan was shaped by Khatami's new approach. From the perspective of Iranian pragmatists, the United States and Iran had converging interests in Afghanistan. They both opposed Taliban rule and desired a stable and relatively strong central government in Kabul. Furthermore, Iran's perennial Afghan problems—including narcotics production, border insecurity, and refugees—were of concern to the United States as well.

However, the Khatami government's policies failed to produce the desired outcome. The George W. Bush administration spurned Iran's efforts of further cooperation in Afghanistan, and instead branded Iran as a member of the Axis of Evil (the other members being Iraq and North Korea).[31] The U.S. government appeared to adopt a policy of regime change toward Iran; Washington may have felt confident that this would work given its successful overthrow of the Taliban in 2001 and Saddam Hussein in 2003.[32]

The negative U.S. reaction to Iran's engagement efforts undercut Khatami's political standing in Tehran.[33] Iranian conservatives, including Supreme Leader Ayatollah Ali Khamenei, had long maintained that the correct approach toward the United States was "resistance" rather than diplomatic engagement.[34] Khamenei, the ultimate decision maker in Iran, may have been amenable to Khatami's engagement efforts, but up to a point. The U.S. response to the Iranian overtures appeared to have confirmed his long-standing perception of U.S. intentions, namely that Washington wanted to overthrow his regime rather than engage it.[35]

The initial U.S.-Iranian cooperation in Afghanistan was followed by a long period of distrust and rising tensions. Iran's secretive nuclear activities, the 2005 election of the hard-line Mahmoud Ahmadinejad as president, and Iranian support for Iraqi Shia insurgents fighting U.S. forces brought U.S.-Iran relations to a new low. Cooperation in Afghanistan became a moot point given the increasingly hostile relations between Tehran and Washington.

Nevertheless, Iran has played an overall positive role in Afghanistan. It has supported a strong central government in Kabul. For Iran, a stable and secure Afghan government makes sense. It can help prevent a Taliban takeover of the country and maintain security along Iran's border area. In addition, strong relations with a central government in Kabul allow Iran to exercise influence beyond western Afghanistan and areas with Tajik and Hazara populations.

At the same time, Tehran has created a de facto zone of influence in western Afghanistan, focused on the city of Herat. Iran also has links to warlords and militias that often act inde-

---

[30] "Khatami Speaks of Dialogue Among Civilizations," *Iranian Diplomacy*, October 2, 2010.

[31] George W. Bush, "State of the Union Address," delivered at the U.S. Capitol, Washington, D.C., January 29, 2002.

[32] David Hastings Dunn, "'Real Men Want to Go to Tehran': Bush, Pre-emption and the Iranian Nuclear Challenge," *International Affairs*, Vol. 83, No. 1, 2007.

[33] For reactions in the Clinton administration toward Khatami's outreach, see Shah Alam, "The Changing Paradigm of Iranian Foreign Policy Under Khatami," *Strategic Analysis*, Vol. 24, No. 9; and Bruce O. Riedel, "The Clinton Administration," *The Iran Primer*, United States Institute of Peace.

[34] Karim Sadjadpour, *Reading Khamenei: The World View of Iran's Most Powerful Leader*, Washington, D.C.: Carnegie Endowment for International Peace, 2009.

[35] Dunn, 2007.

pendently of Kabul. For example, the former warlord Ismail Khan, once the effective ruler of Herat, is known to have close ties to Tehran.[36]

Iran's Positive Economic Influence

Beginning in 2001, Iran's policy toward Afghanistan has demonstrated a desire for stability in its neighbor. Since 2002 Iran has pledged more than $500 million in economic assistance to Afghanistan.[37] Most of that amount has been spent on roads, energy infrastructure, and schools. The Afghan government, particularly President Karzai, view Iran's economic role in Iran as being positive.[38]

Iran is also one of Afghanistan's largest trading partners. Bilateral trade between the two countries reached almost $5 billion by 2013, up from $2 billion in 2011.[39] Although this figure does not seem large by U.S. standards, it nevertheless demonstrates a deep economic relationship between Iran and Afghanistan. Iran exports food products, medicine, oil, and cement to Afghanistan, which is quite dependent on Iran for its oil and fuel needs.[40]

However, trade relations between the two are also lopsided. Iran exports far more to Afghanistan than it imports from its poorer neighbor, as Iranian exports reportedly compose approximately 75 percent of the traded goods.[41] Overall, the trade imbalance between the two countries favors Iran. This is largely due to Afghanistan's weaker economic and industrial base.

In some instances, Iran has used its economic advantage for political effect. The halting of Iranian fuel exports to Afghanistan in the winter of 2010–2011, which had a negative impact on the average Afghan, appears to have been an attempt to pressure U.S. forces and ISAF in Afghanistan.[42]

But overall, Iran's trade relations with Afghanistan serve a positive purpose. In addition to the benefits of bilateral trade, Iran is helping other regional powers develop Afghanistan. For example, India is helping Iran develop the Chabahar port on the Oman Sea in order to facilitate Indian trade with Afghanistan and Central Asia.[43] Chabahar will be linked to Afghanistan by roads and railways being built by Iran and India.[44]

The Iranian-Indian endeavor is no doubt motivated by geopolitics; New Delhi wants to bypass Pakistan and build better relations with Afghanistan, and Kabul wants to diversify the country's trade routes and become less dependent on Pakistan. It is possible that Chabahar

---

[36] Thomas H. Johnson, "Ismail Khan, Herat, and Iranian Influence," *Strategic Insights*, Vol. 3, No. 7, July 2004.

[37] Abrahim Abbasi and Majid Ranjbardar, "Komak-haye Mali-e Iran be Afghanistan: Ahdaf va Asar-e Eqtesadi-ye an" ["Financial Assistance to Afghanistan: Goals and Economic Effects of It"], *Foreign Relations Quarterly*, No. 3, Fall 1990.

[38] Afghan media leader, interview with the authors, February 23, 2013.

[39] Ladane Nasseri, "Iran, Afghanistan Trade Hits $2 Billion in 2011, IRNA Reports," Bloomberg, December 25, 2011.

[40] Frederick W. Kagan, Kimberly Kagan, and Danielle Pletka, *Iranian Influence in the Levant, Iraq, and Afghanistan*, Washington, D.C.: American Enterprise Institute, 2008.

[41] Ibid.

[42] Ray Rivera, "Afghanistan Strained by Shortages as Iran Tightens Flow of Fuel," *The New York Times*, January 9, 2011.

[43] Avi Jorisch, "Port of Damaged Goods; India's Dangerous Investment in Iran's Chabahar," *Forbes*, September 16, 2013.

[44] Christine C. Fair, "India and Iran: New Delhi's Balancing Act," *The Washington Quarterly*, Vol. 30, No. 3, Summer 2008.

can draw business away from Karachi, on which Afghanistan is heavily dependent. Pakistan has often taken advantage of geography to pressure Afghanistan.[45] As a prominent Afghan businessman told us: "At the moment, the Pakistanis have made [operating through Karachi] really expensive. It has put pressure on the people and the government of Afghanistan. They take around $500 million of charges in a year. This might force businessmen to use the ports in Chabahar. If this treatment is continued by Pakistan, then not only Chabahar but Bandar Abbas [Iran's biggest port] as well is a good option for us."[46]

Iran's cooperation with India also helps Tehran decrease its international isolation and enhance its regional clout. But the net effect will be beneficial for Afghanistan as well. Its western areas may become more developed, and it will be less economically and politically dependent on Pakistan, a neighbor that the Kabul government typically distrusts. According to an Afghan businessman, "If Iran tries to improve their goods and prevent illegal trade, then our trade might improve with Iran because their goods are better than Pakistan's."[47] Overall, Iran-Afghan economic activities can be compatible with U.S. goals in Afghanistan, especially as the country's economy faces an uncertain future after the 2016 drawdown.

Iran's Anti-U.S. Policies in Afghanistan

Iran's general approach toward Afghanistan has aligned with overall U.S. objectives. However, not all of Iran's activities have been positive for the United States. While initially welcoming American involvement in Afghanistan under the Khatami government, Iran has increasingly grown resentful and weary of the U.S. military presence on its doorstep. This has been exacerbated by increasing U.S.-Iran tensions over the nuclear program. In general, the Islamic Republic—particularly the Revolutionary Guards—opposes any sort of American military presence in Iran's neighborhood.

Specifically, Iran fears that U.S. military forces in Afghanistan can be used against its nuclear facilities. In addition, Tehran has accused the United States of using Afghan territory for espionage and sabotage activities against Iran. The Iranian government claims that the U.S. Predator drone that crashed in Iran in December 2011 entered Iranian airspace via Afghanistan.[48]

Therefore, it is not surprising that Iran has vigorously opposed a long-term U.S. military presence in Afghanistan. The Iranian government attempted to sabotage the U.S.-Afghan strategic agreement, which provides a long-term framework for cooperation after the U.S. drawdown, by pressuring the Afghan Parliament as well as the Karzai government directly.

Tehran has attempted to achieve its aims through financial means; the Iranian government has provided Karzai and his staff millions of dollars in cash over the years.[49]

---

[45] Crises Analysis Group Pakistan's Strategic Studies Center, 1988.

[46] Prominent Afghan businessman, interview with the authors, January 4, 2013.

[47] Ibid.

[48] Nasser Karimi, "Iran Releases Video Allegedly Captured by Crashed US Spy Drone," Associated Press, February 7, 2013.

[49] Dexter Filkins, "Iran Is Said to Give Top Karzai Aide Cash by the Bagful," *The New York Times*, October 23, 2010.

Iran also funds many Afghan politicians and nongovernmental organizations, including Afghan religious figures. According to one former Afghan government official, Iran has provided funding to a number of other prominent Afghan figures, including Mohammed Fahim, a powerful warlord and the Afghan Vice President.[50] Another former Afghan official we interviewed claimed that Iran distributes money to Afghans in order to buy their support for even narrower objectives, such as showing support for Iran's Quds Day (Jerusalem Day) celebration, which marks the Islamic Republic's goal of "liberating" Palestine from the Israeli occupation. According to this official, "No matter who it is, dollars can buy them. Now everyone is getting paid, even though Iran is in economic crisis. They pay everyone."[51]

Iranian pressure on the Afghan government, however, does not always produce the desired results. Tehran failed to persuade Kabul to reject the U.S.-Afghan strategic agreement, which was signed on May 2, 2012. And it is unlikely that Afghanistan will succumb to Iranian pressure to prohibit a long-term, residual U.S. military presence in Afghanistan. For now, Tehran may have to accept a longer-term American and Western military presence in Afghanistan.

Iran has also worked hard to build *soft influence* in Afghanistan, which is at times used to the detriment of U.S. interests. This has meant Iranian support not only for economic and energy infrastructure but also for building and buttressing pro-Iranian schools, mosques, and media centers. Much of this activity centers on western and northern Afghanistan, in addition to Kabul.[52] The Tajik and the Hazara are the main the focus of Iran's influence activities.

The Islamic Republic aims to strengthen the Shia sect in Afghanistan. In particular, Tehran wants to ensure that its revolutionary ideology becomes dominant among the Afghan Shia. Iran has built and renovated dozens of schools throughout Afghanistan. In addition, Iran has provided thousands of books to these schools; many can be considered "benign," or not having an overt political and ideological purpose. But other educational materials distributed by Iran clearly have a political-ideological agenda.[53] Iran's supplying of books to Afghan schools, especially universities, could enhance its overall influence well into the future. As one Afghan leader told us, "If the books that are published in Iran are taken away, Kabul University won't have anything else."[54]

Iran also appears to have possessed a political motivation in building one of the biggest madrassas in Afghanistan. The Khatam-al Nabyeen Islamic University, operated by Grand Ayatollah Muhammad Asef Mohseni, is a prominent landmark in the Afghan capital. Ayatollah Mohseni, one of the most prominent Shia jurisprudents in Afghanistan, is closely linked with Iran; his madrassa serves as a focal point of Iranian influence activities, including the promotion of *velayat-e faghih*.[55] The madrassa can be used to train Afghan Shia, particularly future religious leaders, to follow and espouse the Islamic Republic's ideology.

---

[50] Former senior Afghan government official, interview with the authors, February 24, 2013.

[51] Former Afghan official, interview with the authors, February 20, 2013.

[52] Ahmad Majidyar and Ali Alfoneh, "Iranian Influence in Afghanistan: Imam Khomeini Relief Committee," *Middle East Outlook*, Vol. 4, 2010.

[53] Kagan, Kagan, and Pletka, 2008.

[54] Hussaini Mazari, Afghan religious leader, interview with the authors, January 1, 2013.

[55] Zarif Nazar and Charles Recknagel, "Controversial Madrasah Builds Iran's Influence in Kabul," Radio Free Europe/ Radio Liberty, November 6, 2010.

Of course, not all Afghan Shia clerics follow Iran's dictates; many appear to follow more-quietist clerics opposed to *velayat-e faghih*. However, Iran's religious influence in Afghanistan among the Shia is significant, especially given the number of clerics with close ties to Iran. According to one senior Afghan official, "Some Shia imams, even though they live within the boundaries of Afghanistan, decided to celebrate their Eid [religious holiday] in Iran, one day later than when Afghanistan celebrates."[56]

Iran has also spent significant resources in building its influence within the Afghan media. It funds the Afghan Voice Agency, which, according to one source, distributes funding to other pro-Iranian media outlets.[57] Iran also has close ties to several other Afghan television and print media outlets. According to a former Afghan official, "There are four TV stations that support Iran, such as Tamadon."[58] Many more Afghans appear to watch television than read newspapers; therefore, greater Iranian influence on Afghan television could mean greater Iranian influence over the Afghan population in general.

Iranian influence in Afghan media is so substantial that Persian words are often used in Pashto-language media.[59] A successful Afghan businessman described Iran's soft influence as such: "To me their biggest influence is cultural and educational. When I watch most of the TV channels, I don't understand them because they use Iranian expressions. Another thing is the universities. Iran has a high influence over the universities and education centers."[60] Another Afghan explained that "whereas Pakistan aims to create 'chaos' after the drawdown, the Iranians are looking to expand their cultural presence."[61]

But Iran has not relied on political intrigue and soft power alone in pressuring the United States and the Afghan government. The Iranian government has also provided measured military support to Afghan insurgents fighting U.S. forces, including members of the Taliban.[62]

Iran's Military Aid to Afghan Insurgents

Iran's military aid to the Taliban has included light arms, rifled-propelled grenades (RPGs), and even military training for Taliban forces on Iranian soil.[63] Iran's support for Taliban insurgents has not been as extensive as its support for Shia insurgents, who inflicted thousands of casualties against U.S. forces in Iraq. Iran's military and intelligence ties with the Taliban are also much less significant than ties to other anti-American groups such as the Lebanese Hezbollah.

---

[56] Senior Afghan official, interview with the authors, February 21, 2013.

[57] Afghan official, interview with the authors, February 21, 2013.

[58] Former senior Afghan official, interview with the authors, February 24, 2013.

[59] Afghan religious leader, interview with the authors, January 1, 2013. According to him, the use of Persian is very common in Afghan Pashtun media. For example, *pohantoon* (Pashto for "university") is called *daneshgah* in Persian, and *maidan hawayee* (airport) is called *foroodgah* in Persian.

[60] Afghan businessman, interview with the authors, January 1, 2013.

[61] Afghan media leader, interview with the authors, February 23, 2013.

[62] Former senior Afghan official, interview with the authors, February 20, 2013.

[63] Senior Afghan security official, interview with the authors, January 2, 2013; Sarah A. Carter, "Iran Training Taliban Fighters to Use Surface to Air Missiles," *Washington Examiner*, October 24, 2010.

This may be in part because the Taliban is a Sunni fundamentalist group at odds with Shia Iran. But Tehran's *measured* support for the Taliban may be tied to very specific goals; it could strengthen Iran's credibility with certain Taliban factions, enhance communication with the Pashtun Afghan population, and increase leverage with the Afghan central government without excessively hurting bilateral relations. It also sends a message to the United States: in the event of a military conflict, Iran has the ability to dial up the pressure against U.S. forces in Afghanistan.

Iran's support for Afghan insurgents may also be motivated by Iran's own struggle with Baluchi separatist insurgents. The Sunni Baluch, residing in southeastern Iran, along the areas of Pakistan and Afghanistan bordering Iran, are one of the most oppressed of Iran's ethnic minority groups.[64] Even under the shah, Iranian Baluchistan was undeveloped and resisted central authority.

The Islamic Republic has responded to Baluchi socioeconomic demands with repression, especially under the presidency of Ahmadinejad. Baluchi Sunni clerics have been arrested and at times have been disappeared by security forces.[65] Moreover, Tehran has followed a policy of *Persianization*, in which Farsi-speaking Iranians are placed in large Baluchi cities such as Zahedan.[66]

In recent years, Iranian Baluchistan has experienced a rise in violence. Jundallah, a Sunni extremist Baluchi insurgent group, has been responsible for dozens of attacks against Iranian officials and soldiers, including a suicide bombing in the city of Pishin, which killed several senior Revolutionary Guard commanders.[67]

The Iranian government has consistently claimed that the Baluchi insurgents, including Jundallah, are supported by the United States, in addition to Israel, Saudi Arabia, and Pakistan. Supreme Leader Ayatollah Khamenei even claimed that Iran had obtained intelligence intercepts proving U.S. complicity.[68]

There is no definitive proof that the United States has provided support to Jundallah. But it would not be far-fetched to assume that Israel or Saudi Arabia has provided support to Iranian Baluchis, along with other groups opposed to the Islamic Republic. Israel, widely suspected of carrying out sabotage attacks against Iran's nuclear program—including assassinating Iranian scientists—has reportedly worked with Iranian Kurdish insurgents and the Mujahedin-e Khalq organization.[69] Saudi Arabia also has a history of supporting Sunni forces arrayed against Tehran. The Iranian professor Nasser Hadian has accused Saudi Arabia of creating an insurgent "infrastructure" in minority-inhabited areas such as Baluchistan.[70]

---

[64] Jalil Khoshkho, "Sistan va Baluchestan: Faghr Dirinie va Hasasiyat haye Konuni" ["Sistan and Baluchestan: Long Existing Poverty and Today's Sensitivities"], *Gozaresh Political and Social*, Vol. 127, October 2001.

[65] Amnesty International, *Iran: Human Rights Abuses Against the Baluchi Minority*, September 2007.

[66] Ibid.

[67] "Jundullah Claims Responsibility for Terror Attack," Press TV, October 18, 2009.

[68] Farideh Farhi, "On Khamenei's Response to Obama," *Informed Comment: Global Affairs* (blog), March 22, 2009.

[69] Richard Engel and Robert Windrem, "Israel Teams with Terror Group to Kill Iran's Nuclear Scientists, U.S. Officials Tell NBC News," NBC News, February 9, 2012.

[70] Nasser Hadian, "Nasser Hadian on Why Iran Is Ready," *The Iran Primer*, United States Institute of Peace, September 20, 2013.

Iran perceives that the United States and its proxies are supporting separatist Baluchi violence. Arming the Taliban can be viewed as the countermeasure. Regardless, the scope of Iran's assistance to insurgent groups indicates that it is not due to rogue action. It appears, however, that Iran's military assistance has waned in recent years. This could be due to a number of factors, including backlash from the Afghan government and growing resentment among the Afghan population from the perceived Iranian interference in Afghan affairs.

Challenges to Iranian Influence in Afghanistan

Iran is certainly an influential power in Afghanistan. Its cultural and religious ties to Afghans provide it with a natural source of leverage, more so than distant powers such as the United States, Russia, and India. Iran also maintains strong political ties to the Afghan central government, in addition to powerful militias and warlords; the Iranian and Afghan economies are also closely linked. However, it would be wrong to assume that Iran's influence in Afghanistan is limitless. Many Afghans and even the political elite increasingly view Iran's activities in a negative light.[71] Specifically, Afghans appear to resent Tehran's political pressure against Kabul and its armed support for both progovernment militias and Taliban insurgents. A number of other issues bedevil Iranian-Afghan ties, including disputes over water rights, the narcotics flow from Afghanistan, and the large Afghan refugee population in Iran, the last of which in recent years has become a particular source of contention between the two countries. While Iran may be an influential actor in Afghanistan, it will face significant constraints, even after the majority of U.S. and ISAF troops have withdrawn.

Popular Resistance to Iranian Influence

Iran is not popular among Afghanistan's Pashtun population. Instead, many of the Afghan Pashtun look to Pakistan and Saudi Arabia for political and religious support. More-religious and extremist Afghan Sunnis—among them members of the Taliban—view Shia-dominated Iran as an abomination. Other Afghan minorities, such as the Sunni Baluchis, may be wary due to Iran's poor treatment of its own Sunni minorities, including its own Baluchis.

But even Iran's closest allies, the Shia Hazara, have doubts about Iran's intentions and influence. Many appear to be resistant to the Islamic Republic's revolutionary ideology and model of *velayat-e faghih*. Young Hazara, in particular, are more likely to be drawn to Iran's youth culture, which is often at variance with the Islamic Republic's strict social and religious norms.[72] The Hazara, a relatively well-educated population, may be under no illusion as to the popularity and even viability of the Islamic Republic.

Even the Hazara political elite, including powerful militia leaders, may be resistant to Iran's influence. It appears that Hazara political parties have put some distance between themselves and Tehran. This is probably due to a desire to appear as an independent and indigenous Afghan religious and ethnic group not beholden to foreign powers. But some Hazara leaders

---

[71]   Pakistan appears to be more resented for its heavy influence in Afghanistan, especially for its support of the Taliban, but Afghan opposition to foreign interference also influences perceptions of Iran.

[72]   Afghan scholar, interview with the authors, January 2, 2013.

may also resent Tehran's often-heavy hand in Afghan affairs. One influential Afghan we interviewed said: "I think some of the political leaders from the time of Jihad who are Shia and supporters of Hazara are less attracted to Iran."[73] It is therefore very possible that Iran no longer exercises the kind of influence among the Shia as it did in the Mujahideen era.

The Hazara have developed a political base and network independent of Tehran, and many of them disapprove of the Islamic Republic as a theocratic political system. One influential Afghan analyst stated that Iran "invested heavily on the Hazara by taking them to the religious schools of Iran, hoping that they will become *pairaw-e-velayat-e-faqeh* [followers of the Islamist system of Iran]. However, over time they turned into the most secular individuals Iran had ever encountered instead of becoming what the Iranians had hoped for."[74]

Furthermore, the Hazara have developed close ties to the United States. According to a former senior Afghan official, "Shiites see themselves as needed by Americans. They are closer to America than Iran."[75] The Hazara political leadership is unlikely to depend on its ties to Iran alone, but will look to the United States and the West for support as well.

In addition to skepticism from key sections of the Afghan population, Iran also faces friction with its neighbor over a number of other issues; disputes over water flows from Afghanistan to Iran is one of the most serious.

Water Disputes

Water disputes between Iran and Afghanistan are a constant source of tension, dating to the 19th century. Both countries suffer from a shortage of water, particularly Iran. The eastern Iranian provinces bordering Afghanistan are particularly water challenged.[76] Disputes have centered mostly on the Helmand River, which flows into the Iranian province of Sistan-Baluchistan and is an important water source for populations in both countries. Exacerbated by drought, water-sharing disputes will likely remain a significant sticking point between Tehran and Kabul.

Following more than a century of disputes over the Helmand's water supply, Iran and Afghanistan signed an accord in 1973, which established a means of regulating each country's use of the river.[77] The deal was not be fully implemented, however, due to unrest in Afghanistan and the Iranian Revolution. According to Iranian officials, based on the 1973 Helmand treaty, Iran should receive an annual share of 820 million cubic meters from the Helmand.[78] On the other hand, some Afghans, including a member of parliament, accuse Iran of taking more water than it is entitled to.[79]

---

[73] Influential Afghan, interview with the authors, February 24, 2013.

[74] Afghan scholar, interview with the authors, January 2, 2013.

[75] Former senior Afghan official, interview with the authors, February 20, 2013.

[76] Andrew Houk, "Transboundary Water Sharing: Iran and Afghanistan," Stimson Center, March 22, 2011b.

[77] Bill Samii, "Iran/Afghanistan: Still No Resolution for Century-Old Water Dispute," Radio Free Europe, September 7, 2005.

[78] Ibid.

[79] Former senior Afghan official, interview with the authors, February 20, 2013.

Afghans at times have intentionally completely cut off the Helmand's flow into Iran.[80] Especially vulnerable to Afghan overuse of the Helmand are the almost one million Iranians living near Sistan-Baluchistan's Hamun Lakes, which are fed by the river; local residents rely on the lakes for drinking water, agriculture, and fishing.[81] The locals depend on the lakes to such an extent that, in 2001, residents were forced to abandon 124 villages when the lake dried up as a result of drought.[82]

Afghan development projects have exacerbated the dispute over the Helmand. Iran is concerned that water flow will be constricted further as dams are built to boost Afghanistan's agriculture sector. Meanwhile, Afghan officials accuse Iran of aiding antigovernment insurgents in order to block construction of the dams.[83] The Kamal Khan Dam in Nimroz Province is one such project. Iran is concerned that the dam will limit water flow into Sistan-Baluchistan.[84] In 2011, a captured Taliban commander claimed that Iran had offered him $50,000 to sabotage the dam.[85] Afghan officials also claim that Iran seeks to prevent the construction of the Bakhsh Abad Dam in Afghanistan's Farah Province.[86]

A dispute has also arisen in recent years over the Harirud, which flows from Herat into Iran's Khorasan-e Razavi Province. Around 3.4 million Iranians, including the residents of the large city of Mashhad, rely on the Harirud for water.[87] There, India is involved in the construction of the Salma Dam. While Iran has been accused of attempts to disrupt this project, its overall desire to cooperate with India may temper its reaction during the construction phase.[88]

Unresolved water disputes between the two countries can also affect overall economic relations. A senior Afghan official said: "Iran wants to help us through Bandar Abbas, but there are some conditions to it. For example, the issue that Iran wants to solve is the waters of Afghanistan that go to Iran."[89]

Narcotics Challenge

Iran has one of the highest rates of drug use in the world.[90] According to Islamic Republic statistics, approximately two million Iranians are addicted to drugs, especially to heroin and other opiates.[91] Afghanistan, the world's biggest producer of opium, is the primary source of Iran's drug problem. Iran is Afghanistan's easiest route to lucrative markets in Europe and beyond.

---

[80] Samii, 2005.

[81] Houk, 2011b.

[82] Ibid.

[83] Fatemeh Aman, "Afghan Water Infrastructure Threatens Iran, Regional Stability," *Al-Monitor*, January 7, 2013.

[84] Ibid.

[85] Ibid.

[86] Afghan official, interview with the authors, February 26, 2013.

[87] Houk, 2011b.

[88] Afghan official, interview with the authors, February 26, 2013.

[89] Senior Afghan official, interview with the authors, February 21, 2013.

[90] United Nations Office on Drugs and Crime, *World Drug Report 2012*, Vienna: United Nations, 2012.

[91] "Tehran Battles Drugs, Addiction and Crime," *Al-Monitor*, March 15, 2013.

Hence, much of the Afghan narcotics trade goes through Iran's 936-kilometer porous border with Iran. A current senior Afghan official claimed that "forty percent of the opium that goes through Iran is consumed in Iran."[92] Iran's deteriorating economy has no doubt compounded its drug problem. Iranian youths, who make up the majority of Iran's population, face unemployment and economic stagnation; without much hope, many are attracted to drugs as a temporary solution or escape.[93]

Tehran does not have the resources to completely stop the flow of drugs through its territory, although it expends a great deal of effort. According to the UN, Iran seizes more heroin and opiates than any other country in the world.[94] It has posted thousands of law enforcement and Revolutionary Guard forces along the border, and has even built walls and trenches along much of the area.[95] The Iranian government claims that more than 3,700 of its forces have been killed and 12,000 injured in clashes with drug smugglers over the past three decades.[96]

According to captured insurgents, the Taliban derives the majority of its funding from poppy proceeds.[97] As of 2008, that amounted to around $50 million per year.[98] Despite initial successes following its 2008 efforts to counter poppy cultivation, ISAF has ultimately been unsuccessful in stemming drug production in Afghanistan. According to the UN, poppy cultivation in Afghanistan has increased for three years in a row, and the country provides 75 percent of the world's supply of heroin.[99]

To date Iran and Western forces in Afghanistan have not fully worked together to counter narcotics. The main reason for this appears to be U.S.-Iran tensions surrounding the nuclear program. However, Iran has been a significant part of the effort to counter the Afghan drug trade. Since 2008, Tehran has housed the Joint Planning Cell of the Triangular Initiative, a UN-facilitated forum in which Iran, Pakistan, and Afghanistan share intelligence regarding drug trafficking and carry out joint interdiction operations.[100]

Despite these joint efforts, however, Iran and Afghanistan do not always see eye to eye on the issue. Tehran regularly complains about the drug trade, often insinuating that this is due to Kabul's inattention or unwillingness to address the issue.[101] But it may be that Kabul does not have adequate resources to do much about border security.

And to be sure, corruption in both Iran and Afghanistan is a major issue. The Karzai government has been roundly criticized for corrupt practices, including associations with the drug trade at the highest level.[102] In Iran, there are indications that some government officials may

---

[92] Senior Afghan government official, interview with the authors, February 26, 2013.

[93] "Tehran Battles Drugs, Addiction and Crime," 2013.

[94] United Nations Office on Drugs and Crime, 2012.

[95] Thomas Erdbrink, "The West's Stalwart Ally in the War on Drugs (Yes, That Iran)," *The New York Times*, October 11, 2012.

[96] "Iran on 'Frontline' of Fight Against Drug Smuggling," *Al Arabiya*, June 26, 2013.

[97] Gretchen Peters, *How Opium Profits the Taliban*, Washington, D.C.: United States Institute of Peace, 2009.

[98] Ibid.

[99] Rod Nordland, "Production of Opium by Afghans Is up Again," *The New York Times*, April 15, 2013.

[100] Andrew Houk, "Iran's Response to Drugs from Afghanistan," Stimson Center, January 28, 2011a.

[101] Erdbrink, 2012.

[102] James Risen, "Reports Link Karzai's Brother to Afghanistan Heroin Trade," *The New York Times*, October 4, 2008.

be involved in the drug trade as well. The U.S. Treasury Department has said that Revolutionary Guard officers are involved in the distribution and sale of narcotics.[103]

It would not be surprising if major elements of the Revolutionary Guards are profiting from narcotics. Iranian officials, including the now-imprisoned reformist leader Mehdi Karroubi, have accused the guards of being involved in illicit activities.[104] According to Karroubi, the guards command dozens of jetties through which they control smuggling. Other officials, including Ahmadinejad (once closely associated with the Revolutionary Guards), have also hinted at their involvement in illicit activities.[105]

Despite these challenges, a joint Iranian-Afghan-American effort (including other partners from ISAF) does have the potential to put a dent in the drug trade. The central governments in Iran and Afghanistan are broadly in support of drug eradication, despite the level of corruption in both countries.

When asked about Iran's interests regarding Afghan drug production, a former Afghan official remarked: "I think the drug economy in Afghanistan will be expanding. The issue of drugs between Afghanistan and the U.S. will be elevated because we will have more production of drugs for export. Therefore there will be a corresponding reaction from Iran on that issue."[106]

Refugee Issues

The status of Afghan refugees in Iran will continue to be a source of tension between Tehran and Kabul following the ISAF withdrawal. According to the UN, Iran houses 868,200 Afghan refugees.[107] However, this number accounts only for those who are documented, so the number is likely much higher. After Pakistan, Iran has taken in more Afghan refugees than any other country in the world.

Around 70 percent of Afghan refugees in Iran are Hazara and Tajiks.[108] Most live in urban areas, with only 3 percent living in refugee settlements.[109] Refugees began flooding into Iran in the late 1970s following the Afghan revolution and the subsequent Soviet invasion of Afghanistan.[110]

---

[103] Samuel Rubenfeld, "Treasury Sanctions Iranian General for Afghan Heroin Trafficking," *The Wall Street Journal*, March 7, 2012.

[104] "Hameh kesani ke be sepah esteham zadanad" ["All the People Who Accused the Revolutionary Guards"], *Mehr News Magazine*, February 28, 2013.

[105] Alireza Nader, "Ahmadinejad vs. the Revolutionary Guards," *The Iran Primer*, United States Institute of Peace, July 11, 2011.

[106] Former senior Afghan official, interview with the authors, January 1, 2013.

[107] Ami Sedghi, "UNHCR 2012 Refugee Statistics: Full Data," *The Guardian*, June 19, 2013.

[108] "Afghan Refugees in Iran & Pakistan," European Resettlement Network, 2013.

[109] Ibid.

[110] Arne Strand, Astri Shurke, and Kristian Berg Harpviken, *Afghan Refugees in Iran: From Refugee Emergency to Migration Management*, Oslo: Chr. Michelsen Institute, June 2004.

Relative to today, refugees were originally treated well by the Islamic Republic.[111] Afghans were allowed to settle anywhere they found work, were provided health care and subsidized food, and their children were provided basic education.[112] Following a brief period of repatriation in 1992 and 1993—after the collapse of Afghanistan's communist government—refugees began returning to Iran once the Taliban took over Afghanistan in 1994.[113] A large portion of this second wave consisted of undocumented immigrants.

In the past decade, the status of Afghan refugees in Iran has deteriorated significantly as a result of both public resentment and government policy. As the Iranian economy has deteriorated—especially in the face of international sanctions—many Iranians appear to resent Afghans, whom they accuse of stealing scarce jobs.[114] The Iranian government also has taken an increasingly hard line against undocumented Afghans. From April to mid-June 2007, Iran deported more than 100,000 undocumented Afghan immigrants—a drastic increase compared with the deportations in all of 2006—fewer than 150,000.[115] In 2012, Iranian officials stated plans to repatriate 900,000 Afghan refugees by 2015.[116]

In Afghanistan, protests have erupted in recent years in response to the poor treatment and, at times, physical abuse of Afghans at the hands of Iranian authorities.[117] There have even been instances of legal refugees being deported.[118] Furthermore, many Afghans in Iran complain that their children are now prevented from receiving an education. And in some cities, officials have prevented Afghans from entering public parks.[119] As of the end of 2012, 19 of Iran's 31 provinces were designated as no-go areas for Afghans by the Iranian government.[120] Due to the poor situation for Afghan refugees in Iran, some have begun moving on to Turkey. According to the UN, as of February 2013, most of the 20,000 Afghan refugees living in Turkey had come in recent months.[121]

The Iranian government frequently uses the refugee issue as a means of pressuring the Afghan government.[122] In 2012, an Afghan official complained that Iran's ambassador to Kabul had warned him that Iran would rapidly deport Afghan refugees if Karzai signed a security pact with the United States.[123] As Afghanistan signed the agreement, it met with Iranian and

---

[111] Ibid.

[112] Ibid.

[113] Ibid.

[114] Ibid.

[115] Alisa Tang, "Iran Forcibly Deports 100,000 Afghans," Associated Press, June 15, 2007.

[116] "Refugee Matters in Iran," Norwegian Refugee Council report, Vol. 1, No. 6, December 2012–January 2013.

[117] "Afghans Demonstrate Against Iranian 'Ill-Treatment,'" BBC News, May 6, 2010; Tang, 2007.

[118] Strand, Shurke, and Harpviken, 2004.

[119] "Afghan Refugees Pin Their Hopes on Rouhani," Deutsche Welle, July 31, 2013.

[120] Amie Ferris-Rotman, "Iran Pushes Out Afghans as Regional Power-Play Heats Up," Reuters, December 2, 2012.

[121] Thomas Seibert, "Afghan Refugees Leave Iran for Turkey," *The National*, February 17, 2013.

[122] Ferris-Rotman, 2012.

[123] Ben Farmer, "Iran Threatens to Expel Afghan Refugees If Kabul Ratifies US Strategic Partnership," *The Telegraph*, May 10, 2012.

UN officials in January 2013 to plan for the voluntary repatriation of 100,000 Afghan refugees by March 2014.[124]

Iran is unlikely to follow through on its repeated threats to deport vast numbers of Afghan refugees. Doing so would greatly harm Iran-Afghan relations. It is estimated that around $500 million per year is injected into Afghanistan's economy in the form of remittances from Iran; mass deportations would have a disastrous impact on Afghans' livelihood.[125] Some Afghans have expressed hope that the plight of refugees in Iran will improve in light of Rouhani's election.[126] Some also likely would prefer to stay in Iran rather than return to an Afghanistan transitioning into an uncertain post-2016 environment.[127]

In conclusion, Iran maintains significant cultural, political, and economic influence in Afghanistan, which can be used to protect Iranian interests after the U.S. drawdown. These interests include thwarting Taliban domination of Afghanistan, countering the flow of narcotics, and protecting Iran's claims to water resources. Depending on the nature of U.S.-Iran relations at the time, Iran could also attempt to undermine any residual U.S. military presence in Afghanistan. However, Iran's influence should not be exaggerated. Iranian influence is constrained by Afghan popular resistance to what is often viewed as Iranian interference in Afghan affairs. Even important Iranian partners such as the Hazara are wary of Iranian intentions.

---

[124] "Refugee Matters in Iran," 2012–2013.

[125] Strand, Shurke, and Harpviken, 2004.

[126] "Afghan Refugees Pin Their Hopes on Rouhani," 2013.

[127] "Refugee Matters in Iran," 2012–2013.

CHAPTER THREE

Iran and Other Powers in Afghanistan

As the Islamic Republic of Iran prepares for the withdrawal of U.S. forces and ISAF from Afghanistan in 2016, the strategy it pursues will be influenced in large part by the actions of Pakistan, India, and Russia. While the new Iranian president, Hassan Rouhani, has promised to usher in an era of nonconfrontational and constructive relations with nations both near and far, the extent to which Tehran will cooperate or clash with Islamabad, New Delhi, and Moscow in Afghanistan depends on the nature of the broader relations it holds with these governments and, in turn, their relations with the United States and each other.

The post-ISAF withdrawal strategy of Pakistan, the state most involved in Afghanistan in recent decades, will shape the course of action that Iran and India take in the country. Both governments intend to limit Pakistani influence over the Kabul administration as a means of containing Islamabad's regional power. If the security situation in Afghanistan were to worsen, Iran-Pakistan relations likely would deteriorate, as each would revert to backing their respective allied militant groups. In the event of a peaceful transition following the troop withdrawal, Iran and Pakistan would be inclined, in the short term, to maintain their current state of cordial relations, largely due to the latter's need for Iranian energy resources to help overcome crippling electricity shortages. In the long term, however, Iran's increasingly close relations with India, as well as sectarian and ethnic tensions between Tehran and Islamabad, could strain relations.

The trajectory of India-Iran cooperation in Afghanistan is set to follow the steady trend of strengthened bilateral ties. Barring open conflict between Iran and India's Arab allies in the Persian Gulf, the two countries are most likely to become closer. This is due to a broad alignment in interests. Since India continues to develop and since energy-rich Iran remains desperate to reach outside markets—coupled with their shared desire to balance against Pakistan—each state would ultimately benefit from an increase in regional influence of the other. This is likely to remain the case despite Washington's efforts to limit New Delhi's ties with Tehran.

Russian activities in Afghanistan will continue to closely align with Iranian and Indian objectives. All four countries have a strong interest in countering the spread of Sunni extremism in the region. Pakistan, on the other hand, has historically supported Sunni extremist groups as a means of maintaining strategic depth and pressuring India. The Kremlin is interested in limiting Pakistan's influence in Afghanistan as Islamabad works closely there with China, Russia's competitor for economic and political power in Central Asia.

Russian-Iranian relations, however, are unlikely to prove as steady as Iran's ties with India. Tehran is wary of Moscow's intentions regarding a range of issues. Moreover, as energy resource exporters, both countries are potential competitors in the global energy market, and thus Russia prefers to see Iran remain a junior partner isolated in the international community. Nevertheless, Iran's marriage of convenience with the Russians in Afghanistan and Central Asia will hold given common security concerns.

Iran and Pakistan

Iran's relations with Pakistan can be characterized as a complex mix of cooperation and peer rivalry. In recent years, political ties between the two countries have improved over trade and energy issues; they also cooperate intermittently on border security. At the same time, tensions continue to exist over religious sectarian issues. As the two continue to compete for political influence in Afghanistan as a means of securing their respective security and economic interests, Pakistan's activities will be a key determinant of Iran's strategy. An increase in unrest brought about by a precipitous withdrawal of ISAF troops from Afghanistan would complicate relations. In the near term, however, tensions will likely be tempered by Pakistan's reliance on Iran for energy.

Iran's relations with Pakistan and India in the mid-20th century were the mirror image of that which exists today. Whereas Tehran now sees New Delhi as a natural partner, it maintained much closer ties with Islamabad throughout most of the Cold War. Iran's last shah, Mohammad Reza Pahlavi, was the first world leader to recognize Pakistan as an independent country in 1947, and he strengthened relations with the new state following the Indian government's decision to support Iran's Egyptian rival, Gamal Abdel Nasser.[1] Bilateral relations were further improved by the 1955 Baghdad Pact, which brought both Iran and Pakistan into the anti-Soviet bloc allied with the United States.

Iran later interceded on Pakistan's behalf during the latter's conflicts with India in 1965 and 1971, providing diplomatic and financial support.[2] Throughout the 1970s, the two countries' militaries and intelligence agencies also cooperated closely to counter the shared threat of Baluchi nationalism. Concerned over the potential effects on Iran's own Baluchi minority, the shah assisted in putting down a separatist insurgency in Pakistan's Baluchistan province.[3]

The 1979 Iranian Revolution greatly altered the nature of Iran-Pakistan relations, transforming the two countries into rivals rather than partners. While Pakistan remained neutral during the Iran-Iraq War, which threatened the fledgling Islamic Republic's existence, Ayatollah Ruhollah Khomeini's efforts to export the Iranian revolution fueled tensions in Pakistan between its Sunni majority and sizable Shia minority.[4] Coinciding with the Pakistani leader Muhammad Zia-ul-Haq's efforts to Islamize the country—an effort that Pakistan's Shia feared would strengthen Sunni extremists—and Saudi funding of Sunni fundamentalist schools, the

---

[1]   Harsh V. Pant, "Pakistan and Iran's Dysfunctional Relationship," *Middle East Quarterly*, Spring 2009.

[2]   Arif Ansar, "Future of Pakistan-Iran Ties," *Pakistan Today*, January 27, 2013.

[3]   Ibid.

[4]   With upward of 26 million Shias living in Pakistan, the community composes almost 15 percent of the country's population. It also makes up about 15 percent of the world's Shia population. Janne Bjerre Christensen, *Strained Alliances: Iran's Trouble Relations to Afghanistan and Pakistan*, Copenhagen: Danish Institute for International Studies, 2011; Pew Forum on Religion and Public Life, *Mapping the Global Muslim Population: A Report on the Size and Distribution of the World's Muslim Population*, Washington, D.C.: Pew Research Center, 2009.

period from the early 1980s to the mid-1990s has been described by the analyst Alex Vatanka as the "zenith of the Islamic Republic's championing of Shia militancy in Pakistan."[5]

In 1986, Khomeini issued a fatwa instructing the Iranian government to protect Pakistan's Shia, which led to the founding of Shia extremist groups such as Tehrik-e-Jafaria.[6] Meanwhile, anti-Shia groups such as the Sepah-e Sahaba began to sprout, targeting Shia doctors, businessmen, and intellectuals.[7] The Iran-Pakistan rivalry intensified further following the 1989 Soviet withdrawal from Afghanistan. In the ensuing civil war, the Pakistani-backed Taliban fought the Iranian-supported Northern Alliance, with the former eventually gaining control over 90 percent of Afghanistan.[8]

Despite the Sunni-Shia violence inside Pakistan and the rivalry in Afghanistan, Islamabad and Tehran maintained ties during the late 1980s and 1990s. Perhaps surprisingly, this period of tension coincided with cooperation between Pakistan and Iran in the field of nuclear technology. The two countries are believed to have signed a nuclear cooperation agreement in 1986, and several Iranian scientists received training in Pakistan in 1988.[9] Meanwhile, the A. Q. Khan network was supplying centrifuge technology for uranium enrichment to the Islamic Republic.[10]

Current Economic and Diplomatic Relations

Ties between Iran and Pakistan have improved over the last decade—driven by political transformations in Tehran as well as economic factors—although tensions could increase over Afghanistan and sectarian issues as well as Iran's closer relations with India.

Following his 1997 election, the reformist president Mohammad Khatami's diplomatic outreach helped pave the way for his December 2002 trip to Islamabad, which marked the first time an Iranian leader had visited Pakistan in a decade.[11] Two years later, the two countries signed a preferential trade agreement, which led to a boost in economic ties.[12] The trade balance has remained in Iran's favor, with Pakistan importing $572 million in goods in 2010-

[5]   Alex Vatanka, "The Guardian of Pakistan's Shia," *Current Trends in Islamist Ideology*, Vol. 13, 2012.

[6]   Ibid.; Robert M. Shelala II, Nori Kasting, and Anthony H. Cordesman, *U.S. And Iranian Strategic Competition: Afghanistan, Pakistan, India, and Central Asia*, working draft, Washington, D.C.: Center for Strategic and International Studies, 2012.

[7]   Hassan Abbas, *Pakistan's Drift into Extremism: Allah, the Army, and America's War on Terror*, Armonk, N.Y.: M.E. Sharpe, 2005.

[8]   Relations soured further in 1990, when Iranian Consul General Sadeq Ganji was assassinated in Lahore. Pant, 2009; Kaveh L. Afrasiabi, "The Iran-Pakistan Nexus," *Asia Times Online*, January 13, 2006.

[9]   Sharon Squassoni, "Closing Pandora's Box: Pakistan's Role in Nuclear Proliferation," *Arms Control Today*, April 2004.

[10]   Some, including A. Q. Khan and former Pakistani Prime Minister Benazir Bhutto, have alleged that several senior Pakistani officials knowingly allowed the transfers to take place, perhaps driven by anti-American sentiment. Although this has not been proven conclusively, the fact that the Pakistani government maintains tight control over the nuclear industry lends credence to the notion that such activities could not have occurred without the complicity of at least some officials. Richard Cronin, Alan Kronstadt, and Sharon Squassoni, *Pakistan's Nuclear Proliferation Activities and the Recommendations to the 9/11 Commission: I.S. Policy Constraints and Options*, Washington, D.C.: Congressional Research Service, 2010; Squassoni, 2004.

[11]   Pant, 2009.

[12]   Whereas in 2004 bilateral trade stood at around $376 million, it had reached $1.3 billion by 2009. Christensen, 2011; Afrasiabi, 2006; "Pakistan Calls for More Trade with Iran," *Tehran Times*, November 20, 2012.

2011, mostly in the form of petroleum, chemical compounds, and machinery.[13] During the same period, Iran imported $162 million in Pakistani goods, mainly rice, fruit, and cotton.

Pakistan's debilitating energy shortage has played a significant role in drawing it closer to Iran, with parts of the country having significantly relied on Iranian electricity since 2002.[14] Key to fulfilling Pakistan's energy needs is the $1.5 billion Iran-Pakistan pipeline, which is intended to transport natural gas from Iran's South Pars gas field to Pakistan's Baluchistan and Sindh provinces.[15] After years of delay—due in part to U.S. pressure on Pakistan to back out of the deal—the two countries signed a $7.6 billion agreement in March 2010, covering pipeline construction as well as Iran's provision of 750 million cubic feet of gas per day upon completion.[16] Further illustrating the Islamic Republic's strong interest in pursuing the project, the Ahmadinejad government announced in January 2013 that Iran would lend Pakistan $250 million in assistance for the construction of the Pakistani portion of the pipeline.[17] According to the deal, the pipeline was expected to be operational by December 2014, with Pakistan anticipating annual royalties ranging anywhere from $500 to 600 million.[18] In December 2013, however, officials from the new Rouhani government announced that Iran would not be providing Pakistan with the loan due to financial strain resulting from sanctions.[19] Iran's deputy oil minister also complained that the pipeline would likely not be operational for another four years due to delays on the Pakistani side. It remains to be seen whether Iran would again offer financing if sanctions were eased.

In any event, some Iranian and Pakistani analysts have remained skeptical throughout the project's lifetime. They believe that Islamabad's recent expressions of eagerness to pursue the deal were simply a political stunt by President Asif Ali Zardari and his supporters to gain popularity with an electorate angry over electricity shortages. Iranians also fear that Pakistan would be quick to drop the project if presented with lucrative incentives from the United States.[20]

Despite efforts by both countries to maintain strong economic ties, international sanctions on Iran have had a negative impact on bilateral trade, which dropped from $1.3 billion in 2009 to $735 million in 2011, largely as a result of U.S. efforts to prevent oil-related transactions with the Islamic Republic.[21] Islamabad and Tehran have attempted to mitigate the impact with workarounds. In 2012, for instance, Iran agreed to barter oil, metals, and fertilizer for foodstuffs from Pakistan as a means of bypassing sanctions and to counter the effects of

---

[13] "Iran-Pakistan Trade Rises Despite U.S. Sanctions," Press TV, March 17, 2012.

[14] By February 2012, Iran was providing Pakistan with 70 megawatts of electricity, with Islamabad pressing Tehran for an additional 1,100 megawatts. In May 2013, Iran announced plans to export $3 million worth of electricity to Pakistan's Baluchistan province per month. Afrasiabi, 2006; Shelala, Kasting, and Cordesman, 2012.

[15] "Iran Funds Gas Pipeline to Pakistan," Press TV, January 30, 2013.

[16] "Iran and Pakistan Sign 'Historic' Pipeline Deal," BBC News, March 17, 2010.

[17] "Iran Funds Gas Pipeline to Pakistan," 2013.

[18] "Iran to Accept Wheat, Meat, Rice as Payment for Fuel," Reuters, February 21, 2013; Christensen, 2011.

[19] "Iran Cancels Pakistan Gas Pipeline Loan," Associated Press, December 14, 2013.

[20] Alex Vatanka, "Problems in the Pipeline: Energy-Starved Pakistan Looks to Iran for Natural Gas," *The Majalla*, May 2, 2013.

[21] "Pakistan Calls for More Trade with Iran," 2012.

the Iranian rial's devaluation.[22] Pakistani rice traders were greatly benefiting from this situation until India regained its position as Iran's main source of rice imports the following year.[23]

Although Pakistan relies on Iran for energy, the two countries could find themselves at odds in the future over their ports in Gwadar (Arabian Sea) and Chabahar (Gulf of Oman). Lying only approximately 100 miles (161 kilometers) apart, Pakistan's Gwadar and Iran's Chabahar are both set to be major transshipment hubs for products moving in and out of Central Asia. The extent to which the ports become a source of tension may depend on whether Pakistan deems Indian involvement in developing Chabahar, which India plans to use as a conduit for goods to Afghanistan and Central Asia, to be part of an effort to limit Islamabad's economic and military presence in the region. For Pakistan, Gwadar provides its navy with strategic depth because it is located farther away than the port of Karachi from India's naval bases in Gujrat and Mumbai.[24]

Gwadar also provides an opportunity for Pakistan to increase its military ties with China: Beijing plans to use the port as a base for its navy, allowing it to bypass the Strait of Malacca and perhaps one day station its forces close to the strategic Strait of Hormuz.[25] As of yet, however, Pakistan and Iran have not expressed concern over a potential rivalry stemming from activities at Gwadar and Chabahar. In fact, in addition to assisting in the construction of an oil refinery in Gwadar, Iran is developing the port's power grid.[26] The two countries even have discussed connecting the ports.[27]

Border stability represents another avenue of cooperation between Iran and Pakistan. With the entirety of their more-than-800-kilometer-long shared border inhabited by Baluchis, Tehran and Islamabad are concerned over their respective Baluchi insurgencies as well as the drug trafficking that helps fund them. Since 2002, the Pakistani-Iranian Joint Ministerial Commission has been meeting to discuss these issues.[28]

Despite their ethnic affiliation, Baluchi populations in each country hold varying grievances, and the nature of their insurgencies differ. In Pakistan, Baluchi insurgents generally are ethnic nationalists whose grievances revolve around lack of development in spite of the resource richness of their province.[29] On the Iranian side of the border, the Baluchi insurgency

---

[22] Tom Arnold, "Iran Looks to Pakistan for Food Deal," *The National*, April 23, 2012.

[23] In February 2013, Iran also announced that it would accept wheat, meat, and rice in exchange for helping Pakistan build an oil refinery in Gwadar. In July of the same year, Iran agreed to accept wheat from the Pakistani government as partial payment for the $51 million Pakistan owes in imports of Iranian electricity. Daniel Fineren, "India Trumps Pakistan's Iran Rice Trade Boom with Oil Rupees," Reuters, March 8, 2013; "Iran to Accept Wheat, Meat, Rice as Payment for Fuel," 2013; N. Umid, "Iran Agrees to Barter Wheat from Pakistan," *Trend*, July 13, 2013.

[24] Hasan Yaser Malik, "Strategic Importance of Gwadar Port," *Journal of Political Studies*, Vol. 19, No. 2, 2012.

[25] Ibid.

[26] Pepe Escobar, "All Aboard the New Silk Road(s)," Al Jazeera, September 16, 2012.

[27] Ibid.

[28] Out of the approximately eight million Baluchis living in the Iran-Pakistan-Afghanistan triborder area, six million live in Pakistan, while between one and two million live in Iran. Afrasiabi, 2006; Alireza Nader and Joya Laha, *Iran's Balancing Act in Afghanistan*, Santa Monica, Calif.: RAND Corporation, 2011.

[29] Between 2003 and 2007, Baluchi insurgents in Pakistan killed around 300 people in 1,700 attacks. Christensen, 2011.

has taken on a jihadist, anti-Shia tone in response to the Islamic Republic's discrimination against Iran's Sunnis, of which Baluchis compose a large portion.[30]

A shared Baluchi threat, however, has not prevented diplomatic spats from arising between Iran and Pakistan, with Tehran criticizing Islamabad for not cracking down extensively enough on the Baluchi jihadist group Jundallah's bases located on the latter's side of the border. In 2009, following a high-profile Jundallah bombing in Iran's Sistan-Baluchistan province that killed several senior members of the Revolutionary Guards, Iran closed its border crossing to Pakistan for several months.[31] Then-President Ahmadinejad openly accused "certain officials in Pakistan" of supporting the insurgents on behalf of the United States.[32] Tensions eased as a result of the February 2010 capture of the Jundallah chief Abdolmalek Rigi, probably due to the assistance of Pakistani intelligence.[33] But the March 2014 kidnapping of Iranian soldiers by Pakistan-based Baluchi insurgents brought tensions between Iran and Pakistan to a new high.

Afghanistan likely will remain the greatest source of competition between Iran and Pakistan. Despite close economic cooperation, mutual suspicion exists over developments there. According to Ahmed Rashid, "Whatever their official line might be, beneath the surface the intelligence agencies of both these countries are extreme rivals."[34] This is a result of divergent interests, rendering "leverage within Afghan politics . . . a zero-sum game."[35]

Islamabad worries, for instance, that a strong anti-Pakistani government in Kabul would begin asserting itself over the Durand Line issue, a border dispute between the two countries that remained dormant during Taliban rule.[36] Iran, on the other hand, fears the return to rule of the Pakistani-backed Taliban. Since NATO forces ousted the Taliban government in 2001, the Pakistani city of Quetta has served as its capital in exile.[37] Meanwhile, Iran and Pakistan both compete for the hearts and minds of Afghanistan's educated class by offering study opportunities in their respective centers of learning.[38]

In the end, however, Afghanistan is more central to Pakistan's core national interests than it is to Iran's.[39] Whereas Iran has direct access to Central Asian markets through its border with Turkmenistan, Pakistan's most direct route goes through Afghanistan.[40] Pakistan also sees Afghanistan as an essential means of maintaining "strategic depth" in its rivalry with India. Meanwhile, Iran will likely continue placing most of its focus on projecting power in

---

[30] Since the 2003 founding of Jundallah by Baluchi religious extremists, the group and its affiliates have targeted both Iranian security officials and civilians in ambushes and suicide attacks. Chris Zambelis, "Back with a Vengeance: The Baloch Insurgency in Iran," *Terrorism Monitor*, Vol. 9, No. 2, 2011.

[31] Shelala, Kasting, and Cordesman, 2012.

[32] Farhan Bokhari, "Tensions Rise Between Pakistan and Iran," CBS News, October 19, 2009.

[33] Ishaan Tharoor, "Iran's Arrest of an Extremist Foe: Did Pakistan Help?" *Time*, February 25, 2010.

[34] Christensen, 2011, p. 40.

[35] Afghan researcher, interview with the authors, January 4, 2013; "The New Great Game," *The Economist*, Intelligence Unit, January 30, 2013.

[36] Afghan religious leader, interview with the authors, January 1, 2013.

[37] Christensen, 2011.

[38] Influential Afghan, interview with the authors, February 23, 2013.

[39] Afghan scholar, interview with the authors, February 19, 2013.

[40] Nader and Laha, 2011.

the Middle East and the Arab world.[41] As a result, according to a former senior Afghan official, Pakistan's security role in Afghanistan is expected to increase relative to Iran following the ISAF withdrawal.[42] Other Afghan officials and experts also foresee Pakistan's economic influence in the country surpassing Iran's.[43]

This rivalry notwithstanding, neither country's interests would be served by intensified conflict in Afghanistan, which would result in increased refugee flows.[44] According to data published in 2012 by the United Nations High Commissioner for Refugees, Pakistan has taken in more refugees than any other country in the world, followed by Iran.[45] A return to civil war in Afghanistan likely would exacerbate sectarian tensions in the region as well, with Iran backing its Shia allies and Pakistan backing Sunni militants.[46]

A sustained increase in sectarian attacks inside Pakistan also could affect ties between Tehran and Islamabad, although officials in both countries would probably attempt to downplay its impact. In recent years, Tehran has prioritized cordial ties with Islamabad over defending Pakistan's besieged Shias. Vatanka maintains, "Those in charge of the Islamic Republic engage in a clear attempt to paint relations as healthy and to brush aside any factors that might complicate ties."[47] This comes at the cost of upsetting interest groups in both countries. Pakistani Shia activists report being disappointed by the lack of Iranian pressure on the Islamabad government to protect them.[48] Meanwhile, Iranian clerics and the media criticize Iran's government for not doing enough to protect their Shia brethren. For instance, Iranian news outlets have referred to the Pakistani town of Parachinar as "a second Gaza" because of the violence perpetrated by Sunni extremists against its Shia population.[49] While Iranian officials decry the violence, they usually target their criticism toward the U.S. and Saudi governments in order not to upset ties with Pakistan.[50] Iranian leaders may find it difficult to deflect criticism if sectarian violence worsens, however.[51]

Pakistani popular sentiment as a whole could also limit ties. In a 2012 Zogby poll of the Muslim world, 71 percent of Pakistani respondents reported holding an unfavorable attitude

---

[41] Influential Afghan, interview with the authors, February 19, 2013.

[42] Former Afghan official, interview with the authors, February 24, 2013.

[43] Senior Afghan official, interview with the authors, February 21, 2013.

[44] Afghan researcher, January 4, 2013.

[45] Pakistan houses more than 1.6 million refugees, while Iran has 868,200. Moreover, of the 2.6 million Afghan refugees in the world, 95 percent live in Pakistan and Iran. Sedghi, 2013.

[46] Preparing for this potential outcome likely plays into Pakistani security services' calculations regarding the extent to which they are willing to curb the activities of the anti-Shia group Lashkar-e Jhangvi, an offshoot of Sepah-e Sahaba. Several high-level commanders of Tehrik-e Taliban of Pakistan, which supports the Haqqani network, have come from Lashkar-e Jhangvi, highlighting the level of Pakistani militant involvement in Afghanistan. Pant, 2009; M. Ilyas Khan, "Formidable Power of Pakistan's Anti-Shia Militants," BBC News, January 11, 2013.

[47] Vatanka, 2012.

[48] Ibid.

[49] According to Pakistani government figures, from 2007 to the end of 2011, at least 1,000 people were killed in sectarian violence in Parachinar. Vatanka, 2012.

[50] Ibid.

[51] In 2012, Pakistan saw a spike in Shia casualty rates compared with recent years. And as of February 2013, more than 200 Shias had been killed in Pakistan during the year. Khan, 2013.

toward Iran, and only 26 percent thought relations should become closer.[52] Views differed markedly among Sunnis and Shias, however, signifying the great sectarian divide in the country. While only 10 percent of Pakistani Sunnis held a favorable view toward Iran, 94 percent of Shias did. In fact, 81 percent of Shias supported the Iranian government over the anti-Ahmadinejad Green Movement, while the same proportion of Sunnis identified with the protesters.

Future Trends

In the near term, increased U.S. tensions with Pakistan, including over drone strikes and other counterterrorism activities, may push Islamabad closer to Tehran.[53] While Iran is not popular among the Pakistani populace, anti-American sentiment is higher in Pakistan than in any other country in the Muslim world, with 94 percent of Pakistanis holding unfavorable views toward the United States.[54] Iranian officials have played on this sentiment. For instance, in May 2013, Ahmadinejad told a meeting of Pakistani officials that "Pakistan's enemies will be considered the enemy of Iran."[55]

Additionally, the more Islamabad has seen its relations with Washington deteriorate, the more it has counted on Iran for its electricity needs.[56] The United States is keen to provide alternatives to Iranian energy, with plans to complete a project in 2013 to provide 900 megawatts of electricity to approximately two million Pakistanis.[57] However, this source of leverage would decrease if Pakistan's electrical grid and energy market were to become more integrated with Iran's.

Over the long term, serious issues remain between Iran and Pakistan. The ISAF withdrawal from Afghanistan could increase tensions between Iran and Pakistan if it resulted in further instability; the presence of Western troops in Afghanistan has been the main reason for the abatement of the proxy battle between the Pakistani-backed Taliban and the Northern Alliance supported by Iran.

Therefore, with regards to Afghanistan, it is not in Washington's interest to undermine Iran-Pakistan relations. Cooperation between Tehran and Islamabad is essential in dealing with challenges such as drug trafficking and repatriation of refugees, both of which are important factors in maintaining regional stability.[58]

In the event of a stable Afghanistan, the nature of Iran-India cooperation in Afghanistan will influence how Pakistan evaluates its relations with the Islamic Republic. Pakistan most likely will look to its partnership with China as a means of competing with Iranian and Indian projects in Afghanistan. Moreover, if Iran were to escape its current isolation and become less reliant on Pakistan—for instance, in the event of a resolution to its nuclear dispute—officials

[52] *Looking at Iran: How 20 Arab and Muslim Nations View Iran and Its Policies*, Washington, D.C.: Zogby Research Services, 2012.

[53] Shelala, Kasting, and Cordesman, 2012.

[54] *Looking at Iran: How 20 Arab and Muslim Nations View Iran and Its Policies*, 2012.

[55] Meir Javedanfar, "Iran's New Opportunity to Improve Relations with Pakistan," *Al-Monitor*, May 28, 2012.

[56] Reza Sanati, "Pipeline Politics," *Cairo Review of Global Affairs*, July 21, 2013.

[57] Huma Imtiaz, "Iran Pipeline Deal: Pakistan Should Avoid 'Sanctionable Activity,' Says US," *Express Tribune*, February 28, 2012.

[58] Christensen, 2011.

in Tehran could feel more emboldened to criticize Islamabad over sectarian issues or the activities of anti-Iran insurgents in Pakistan's Baluchistan province.

Iran and India

Relations with India have proven to be an important means for Iran to escape international isolation. The two powers share historical and cultural links; Persian was at one time the language of the Moghul court in India, and Bollywood has been a source of influence in Iranian society for some time. In addition, both countries are important members of the Non-aligned Movement and see themselves as developing countries escaping the bonds of past Western imperialism and colonialism.

As one of the world's largest developing economies, India's appetite for energy resources has ensured that New Delhi maintains close ties with Tehran despite U.S. pressure. Coupled with a shared interest in countering Pakistan's regional influence, economic factors will continue to push the two countries closer together over the long term. In Afghanistan, India's cooperation with Iran is mainly premised on its rivalry with Pakistan and its need for an alternate route to Central Asian markets. India also seeks to balance against China, which is close to Pakistan and active in Central Asia.

Iran's relations with New Delhi were limited by Tehran's close ties with Islamabad prior to the 1979 Iranian Revolution. Indian foreign policy during the Cold War, though officially neutral, tended to tilt in favor of the Soviet Union, while Iran and Pakistan were both part of the bloc composing the anti-Soviet Central Treaty Organization (CENTO). Iran-India ties also suffered following the latter's support for the shah's Egyptian rival, Nasser, during the 1950s and 1960s. Meanwhile, Iran sided with Pakistan on its dispute with India over Kashmir.

Two factors dramatically altered Iran-India relations: the Iranian Revolution and the end of the Cold War. As the rise of Khomeini strained Tehran-Islamabad relations, India's ties with Iran improved. This was in spite of the Islamic Republic's continued criticism of Indian actions in Kashmir.[59] The Soviet Union's collapse, and the eventual dominance of the Taliban in Afghanistan, provided further impetus for India to cooperate with Iran in supporting the Northern Alliance as a means of countering Pakistan's regional activities.

Within the last two decades, Iran-India ties have overtaken Iran's ties with Pakistan—despite stabilization in Tehran's relations with Islamabad over the past decade. The change in balance began with Prime Minister Narasimha Rao's visit to Tehran in 1993, which "marked an important landmark" in the development of bilateral relations, and was intended to drive a wedge further between Iran and Pakistan.[60] In April 2001, India and Iran signed a memorandum of understanding on defense cooperation, and two years later, Iranian President Khatami was invited to New Delhi, where the two countries' leaders announced a "vision of a strategic partnership."[61]

When describing the nature of Iran-India ties, officials in both countries have long spoken of a shared cultural heritage dating back centuries. Following Rouhani's June 2013 election as

---

[59] K. N. Tennyson, "India-Iran Relations: Challenges Ahead," *Air Power*, Vol. 7, No. 2, 2012.

[60] Ibid., p. 154.

[61] Ibid., p. 158.

Iran's president, Indian Prime Minister Manmohan Singh reiterated that Iran and India "enjoy deep historical and civilizational links which have provided a strong foundation for [their] broad-based and mutually beneficial relationship."[62] In this vein, India has striven to cultivate its Shia connection to Iran.[63] Importantly for Iran-India ties, Indian Shias are active members of the political elite, holding high-ranking positions in most of the dominant political parties.[64] Furthermore, India sees Iran as an influential Islamic state that can counter Pakistan's anti-India propaganda in the Muslim world.[65]

Current Economic and Diplomatic Relations

India's increasing need for energy resources and its continued rivalry with Pakistan have driven New Delhi to maintain good relations with Tehran. Moreover, as a fellow member of the Non-aligned Movement, India's foreign policy is influenced by national feelings of solidarity with the developing world.[66] Singh's visit to Iran to participate in the August 2012 Non-aligned Movement summit—accompanied by 250 high-ranking Indian officials—illustrated the importance that bilateral relations hold for India.[67] For its part, as the Islamic Republic has become increasingly isolated due to international sanctions, it has come to more heavily rely on India as a source of income from oil exports. According to Elham Nouri, a visiting scholar at the Tehran-based Center for Scientific Research and Middle East Strategic Studies, India's increasing economic and soft power benefits Iran in that India can help the Islamic Republic escape isolation from sanctions.[68] Recognizing this, Rouhani has stated that "expanding relations with India in all areas is among the priorities" of his administration.[69]

In addition to importing Iranian energy resources, India is interested in expanding its exports to Iran, which include tea, rice, pharmaceuticals, automobiles, electronics, spare parts, and agricultural products.[70] In a May 2013 India-Iran Joint Economic Commission meeting, the two countries agreed to expand bilateral trade to $25 billion in the next four years.[71] The Indian private sector's interest in the Iranian market was highlighted in March 2012, when

---

[62] "PM Congratulates Rouhani," *Business Standard*, July 21, 2013.

[63] The 160-million-plus Muslims living in India compose the world's largest minority population. Approximately 15 percent of Indian Muslims are Shia, who in turn make up almost 15 percent of the world's Shia population. Pew Forum on Religion and Public Life, 2009.

[64] For instance, Hamid Ansari, the former vice president, is a Shia. Raja Karthikeya, "India's Iran Calculus," *Foreign Policy*, September 24, 2010.

[65] Tennyson, 2012.

[66] Iranian President Rouhani has also lauded bilateral ties as a force for peace and stability in the region. Elham Nouri, "Taghviyat e ravabat e Iran Va Hind" ["Strengthening of Iran-India Ties and Its Impact on Regional Development and Stability"], Center for Scientific Research and Middle East Strategic Studies, September 17, 2012; "Pasokh Rouhani be payam tabrik enokhost vazir e Hind" ["Rouhani's Response to Messages of Congratulations from Prime Minister of India, Head of Indonesian Parliament, and President of Montenegro"], *Khabar Online*, July 8, 2013.

[67] Nouri, 2012.

[68] Ibid.

[69] "Rouhani's Response to Messages of Congratulations from Prime Minister of India, Head of Indonesian Parliament, and President of Montenegro," 2013.

[70] Meena Singh Roy, "India and Iran Relations: Sustaining the Momentum," ISDA issue brief, Institute for Defence Studies and Analyses, 2013.

[71] That would be up from $16 billion in 2011–2012. Ibid.

70 government officials and businesspeople traveled from India to Iran as part of a delegation of the government-backed Federation of Indian Export Organisations in an effort to boost exports from India to Iran and deepen ties with the Islamic Republic.[72]

It was noteworthy that this occurred less than one month after an alleged Iranian attempt on the life of an Israeli diplomat in New Delhi. India's subdued reaction to revelations of Iranian involvement in the attack signaled the government's desire not to disrupt other aspects of the bilateral relationship.[73] Iran is also interested in attracting Indian investment. In July 2013, for instance, Iran offered three Indian companies lucrative production-sharing contracts in its energy sector.[74] Additionally, Iran is seeking Indian assistance in improving its information technology networks, ports, roads, and railroads.[75]

Despite these overall trends, bilateral relations have experienced periods of strain in recent years as a result of India's position on Iran's nuclear program, a stance that is heavily influenced by U.S. pressure. At the official level, India continues to call for Iran to comply with all International Atomic Energy Agency (IAEA) and UN Security Council resolutions pertaining to its nuclear program, which include the halting of uranium enrichment.[76] India's cooperation with the United States over Iran is, however, a controversial topic within Indian politics. While India does not want to witness a nuclear-armed Iran, many within the Indian political establishment see the Iranian nuclear issue as a means of exercising India's "strategic autonomy"—in other words, its ability to stand up to U.S. calls for New Delhi to distance itself from Tehran.[77]

Nevertheless, U.S. pressure has impacted Iran-India relations in the past. In 2005, at the start of talks between Washington and New Delhi over developing India's civil nuclear industry, the U.S. Congress made clear that it saw approval of a U.S.-India nuclear deal as tied to Indian cooperation over countering Iran's nuclear progress.[78] Acquiescing to U.S. demands, in February 2006, India voted in favor of referring the Iranian nuclear file to the UN Security Council. Iran lashed out, claiming that the U.S.-India civil nuclear deal endangered the Treaty on the Non-proliferation of Nuclear Weapons.[79] In 2009, India also voted in favor of an IAEA resolution censuring Iran's nuclear program.[80] Iran showed its displeasure by resuming criticism of Indian policies in Kashmir, an activity from which it had refrained since the 1990s.[81]

Sanctions on Iran also have complicated its economic and energy relations with India, as officials in Tehran have expressed frustration with what they see as New Delhi's succumbing to pressure from Washington. During his March 2013 trip to India, Iran's Speaker of Parliament Ali Larijani expressed that there had developed "major differences" between India and

---

[72] Farhad Pouladi, "More Iran-India Trade Would Boost Ties: Delegation," AFP, March 10, 2012.

[73] Tennyson, 2012.

[74] This was a landmark shift compared with Iran's previous offer of only 15 percent fixed returns under a buy-back agreement. Sujay Mehdudia, "Sanctions Weigh on India as It Considers Iran's Gas Offer," *The Hindu*, July 14, 2013.

[75] In 2008, India and Iran signed an agreement to establish a railway between Iran and Russia. Tennyson, 2012; Roy, 2013.

[76] "U.S.-India Joint Statement," White House Office of the Press Secretary, September 27, 2013.

[77] Harsh V. Pant, "India's Relations with Iran: Much Ado About Nothing," *Washington Quarterly*, Vol. 34, No. 1, 2011.

[78] Ibid.

[79] Ibid.

[80] Indrani Bagchi, "India Votes Against Iran at IAEA," *Times of India*, November 28, 2009.

[81] Tennyson, 2012.

the Islamic Republic as a result of a backlog in oil payments owed to Iran.[82] And in a May 2013 televised debate, Ali Akbar Velayati, a presidential candidate and foreign policy adviser to Supreme Leader Khamenei, argued that India and China had been using the sanctions to take advantage of Iran, with each holding around $30 billion of Iran's foreign currency reserves.[83]

This is due to obstacles placed on financial transactions with Iran. When in December 2010 India yielded to U.S. pressure in not allowing Indian businesses to use the Asian Clearing Union to conduct transactions for importing oil and gas, the result was a backlog of payments to Iran as India struggled to find alternative means.[84] By 2012, Iran was receiving 45 percent of its payments in rupees, and as of July 2013, India owed Iran more than $1.5 billion in unpaid oil bills, which Iran also agreed to receive in rupees.[85] The piling up of rupees in Iranian bank accounts has been a boon for Indian exporters, making Iran a captive market.[86] For instance, the Iranian Health Ministry has expressed interest in importing 28 different varieties of medicine from India in order to make up for shortages indirectly caused by Western financial sanctions.[87]

Sanctions once again caused a diplomatic row between Iran and India when, on August 13, 2013, the Revolutionary Guards impounded an Indian tanker it claimed was polluting the waters of the Persian Gulf.[88] Iran held the tanker—carrying 140,000 tons of oil from Iraq to India—for days, demanding compensation, but the ship's insurer was European and thus not allowed to compensate Iran because of sanctions.[89]

The sanctions have also stalled projects that would help India diversify its sources of energy. For instance, a $22 billion deal signed between the two countries, in which Iran is slated to supply India with liquefied natural gas (LNG) for 25 years, is in limbo because the deal stipulates that India build an LNG plant in Iran.[90] India's on-again-off-again interest in the would-be Iran-Pakistan-India (IPI) pipeline is yet another example of the complications New Delhi has faced in increasing its economic ties to the Islamic Republic.

The IPI project, the idea of which has been floated since 1989, was originally planned to transport natural gas from Iran through Karachi and on to Delhi.[91] However, India formally withdrew from the project talks in 2008. Iranian commentators at the time accused India of

---

[82] Yogesh Joshi, "As U.S. Leaves Afghanistan, India Reconsiders Iran Policy," *World Politics Review*, May 9, 2013.

[83] Muhammad Sahimi, "Iran Election Roundup: Television and Revelations," Muftah, May 27, 2013.

[84] Jay Solomon and Subhadip Sircar, "India Joins U.S. Effort to Stifle Iran Trade," *The Wall Street Journal*, December 29, 2010.

[85] By August 2013, India planned to settle all its trade with Iran in rupees. "India Mulls Insurance Guarantee for Refiners Using Iran Oil," Reuters, August 8, 2013; Shelala, Kasting, and Cordesman, 2012; "India to Pay in Rupees for Iran's Oil," *Deccan Herald*, July 14, 2013.

[86] India had run an $11 billion trade deficit with Iran in 2011–2012. "Iran Imports Vehicles, Medicines from India to Bypass US-Led Oil Sanctions," Iran's View, May 17, 2013.

[87] In May 2013, Iran also agreed to import Indian vehicles and medicines as part of payments to its oil industry. In 2013, India also resumed its place as Iran's main source of rice imports due to Iran's large holdings of rupees in Indian banks. "Iran Keen to Import Drugs from India," Fars News Agency, January 3, 2013; "Iran Imports Vehicles, Medicines from India to Bypass US-Led Oil Sanctions," 2013; Fineren, 2013.

[88] "India Sends Team to Iran over Tanker," Islamic Republic of Iran Broadcasting, August 20, 2013.

[89] Ibid.

[90] Pant, 2011.

[91] Sanati, 2013.

having played the "Iran card" all along in order to extract concessions from the West.[92] Five years later, however, a "realization has begun to dawn in India that New Delhi is paying a high price by opting out of the IPI pipeline," according to Reza Sanati of Florida International University's Middle East Studies Center.[93] Moreover, with U.S.-India nuclear cooperation currently stalled for a variety of reasons, one of the main sources of leverage compelling India to refrain from the IPI deal is gone.

While attempting to placate the United States, India has been trying to mitigate the impact of sanctions on its relations with Iran. Until recently, Iran had been India's second-largest source of oil, after Saudi Arabia. Although Iran had dropped to seventh place by March 2013, and India had cut its oil imports from Iran by half in June 2013, India clearly still sees Iran as an important long-term source of energy.[94] In order to make up for the challenges caused by European reinsurance companies backing out due to Western sanctions, the Indian Finance Ministry agreed in July 2013 to provide local insurance companies serving Indian refineries with $327 million in insurance guarantees to cover the refining of Iranian oil.[95]

Cooperation in Afghanistan has led to a closer alignment of Iranian and Indian foreign policy, with both countries interested in a Kabul government devoid of Taliban members and independent of Pakistan. The scheduled ISAF drawdown only serves to strengthen the relationship.[96] As a major part of their strategy to lessen Pakistani influence in Afghanistan, Iran and India have engaged in joint development projects in the country. Although New Delhi has shouldered a higher amount of the funding, Tehran's participation is essential in that Iran provides India with a viable route to Central Asian markets and is India's most feasible way of accessing Afghanistan.[97] One high-profile example of Indian-Iranian collaboration in the country is the Delaram-Zaranj Highway, which India spent $84 million to construct.[98] Completed in 2008, the highway connects Afghanistan's Iranian border to the Kandahar-Herat highway. On the Iranian side, the road connects to the strategically important Chabahar port.

The port is so important to India that, in a May 2013 meeting of the India-Iran Joint Economic Commission in Tehran, New Delhi agreed to invest $100 million in a project to expand its capacity.[99] In a further attempt to cement Iran's and India's footholds in the Afghan economy, the two countries' leaders met with Hamid Karzai on the sidelines of the 2012 Non-aligned Movement summit in Tehran to discuss moving ahead with a plan to develop a "south-

---

[92] Ibid.

[93] Ibid.

[94] Prasenjit Bhattacharya, "Iran Slips to 7th Among India's Oil Suppliers," *The Wall Street Journal*, March 15, 2013; "India Mulls Insurance Guarantee for Refiners Using Iran Oil," 2013.

[95] This was spurred by a drop in the value of the rupee, making dollar-priced oil imports more expensive. "India Mulls Insurance Guarantee for Refiners Using Iran Oil," 2013.

[96] Joshi, 2013.

[97] As of May 2013, India had invested around $2 billion in Afghanistan. Ibid.

[98] Eray Basar, *The Roles of India and Pakistan in Afghanistan's Development and Natural Resources*, Norfolk, Va.: Civil-Military Fusion Centre, 2012.

[99] Chabahar, along with a planned railroad project, is essential to the Steel Authority of India's plan to access $1–3 billion of iron ore located in Afghanistan's Hajigak mines. Joshi, 2013; Vijay Prashad, "The Iran-India-Afghanistan Riddle," *Asia Times Online*, August 28, 2012a.

ern silk road," a trade route of railroads and roads through Iran that would connect South Asia to Central Asia and the Gulf of Oman.[100]

Although India and Iran have shared long-term interests in Afghanistan, the two have not seen eye to eye on everything. In western Afghanistan, for instance, India and Iran are at odds over the construction of the Salma Dam over the Harirud River. Once completed, the $200 million Indian development project will increase arable land for Afghan farmers and produce 42 megawatts of electricity.[101] But it also will cut off up to 73 percent of the Harirud's water flow into Iran, upon which population centers in eastern Iran, such as Mashhad, rely.[102] Over the years, Afghan officials have suspected Iran of sabotaging the project.[103] However, Iran's reliance on India for oil revenue likely gives New Delhi leverage to eventually stop Tehran from opposing the dam's construction.[104]

Future Trends

India appears more willing than Pakistan to avoid tensions with the United States by tempering its relations with the Islamic Republic. Indian officials want India to be seen as a responsible rising power. Thus, it is placed in the difficult position of "trying to strike a balance between preserving its strategic interests and adhering to its global obligations."[105] This has contributed to a relatively "underdeveloped relationship" between Tehran and New Delhi, despite the improvement in ties in recent decades.[106]

India also must keep in mind its relations with Iran's rivals in the Middle East. According to Harsh V. Pant, an expert on Asian security issues at King's College in London, India would ultimately choose to preserve its relations with the Gulf Arab countries over its ties to Iran in the event of hostilities in the Persian Gulf.[107] The Persian Gulf monarchies of Saudi Arabia and Qatar are India's most important sources of energy. The role of Saudi Arabia, long serving as India's primary source of oil, as supplier has increased in importance as Iran's oil industry has become isolated due to sanctions.[108]

Meanwhile, Qatar remains India's only supplier of natural gas.[109] On the military front, India maintains stronger defense ties with Saudi Arabia than it does with Iran.[110] India also

---

[100] The Joint Working Group, comprising India, Iran, and Afghanistan, meets every three months to discuss the new route. Vijay Prashad, "Silk Road Nears an Historic Opening," *Asia Times Online*, September 12, 2012b.

[101] Scott Peterson, "Why a Dam in Afghanistan Might Set Back Peace," *Christian Science Monitor*, July 30, 2013.

[102] Ibid.

[103] In 2010, they accused Iran of complicity in the assassination of a local governor who supported the project. Peterson, 2013.

[104] Afghan official, interview with the authors, February 21, 2013.

[105] Harsh V. Pant, "Delhi's Tehran Conundrum," *The Wall Street Journal*, September 20, 2010.

[106] Pant, 2011, p. 62.

[107] Ibid.

[108] India's imports of Iranian oil in 2012–2013 dropped around 27 percent compared with the previous year. Ibid.; Mehdudia, 2013.

[109] Pant, 2011.

[110] In 2010, Singh became the first Indian prime minister to visit Riyadh in 28 years. While there, he referred to the India-Saudi relationship as a "strategic partnership." Approximately 1.5 million Indians work in Saudi Arabia, making it the kingdom's largest expatriate community. Ibid.

manages close relations with Israel; following establishment of full ties in 1992, India has become Israel's top purchaser of arms, having imported about $1 billion worth of Israeli weapons in 2012.[111] Until now, however, Iran has refrained from making public any displeasure over India's ties to its rivals—likely a result of Iran's increasing reliance on India for revenue.

As ISAF troops withdraw from Afghanistan, Iranian and Indian interests will increasingly converge as they attempt to balance against Pakistan.[112] According to A. V. Chandrasekaran, a senior fellow at the Center for Air Power Studies in New Delhi, influence in Afghanistan is an important "element within India's larger desire to be able to protect its interests well beyond South Asia."[113] While the Indians and Iranians have differed over the presence of Western troops in the region—India was in favor of a longer ISAF deployment—officials in both countries are concerned over what they see as Western pressure on Kabul to accept a road map favorable to Pakistan, which would plan for elements of the Taliban incorporated into the Afghan government.[114]

Iran and Russia

Iran's ties with Russia are considerably more complicated than its relations with India or Pakistan. For various historical reasons, Iranians have long been suspicious of Russian intentions and remain hesitant to see Russia as a reliable international partner.[115] Meanwhile, Russia benefits from an isolated Islamic Republic, preferring for Iran to remain a junior partner. The fact that both countries are major exporters of energy also plays into Moscow's long-term Iran strategy; Russia stands to lose in the event of a globally integrated Iran. Currently, however, Tehran and Moscow share an interest in countering a strong U.S. presence in the region. They are also concerned with the spread of Sunni extremism in Central Asia and the Caucasus. As a result, Russia's interests in Afghanistan align most closely with those of Iran and India, both of which seek to prevent the Taliban's resurgence in Kabul. Having fought a bloody, decadelong war in Afghanistan—often called the "Soviet Union's Vietnam"—the Russians maintain a keen interest in the country, because its security situation impacts stability in greater Central Asia.

The Russians and Iranians have experienced a checkered past. From the early 19th century to the middle of the 20th, no outside power other than the British Empire played as consequential a role in Iranian affairs. During the 19th century, Iran fought several wars with tsarist Russia, eventually losing its territories in the Caucasus, including Azerbaijan, Armenia, and Georgia. To this day, Iranians see the Persian Qajars' signing of the Treaties of Golestan and Turkmenchay—ceding the territories to Russia—as a shameful capitulation of sovereignty to outside powers. Further exacerbating the Iranian people's sense of victimization at the hands of foreigners, in 1907, the Russian and British empires carved Iran into two spheres of influence, with the tsar controlling the northern half. During this period, Russia helped quash the

---

[111] Tennyson, 2012.

[112] Karthikeya, 2010.

[113] A. V. Chandrasekaran, "Afghanistan: India's Interests," *Defence and Diplomacy Journal*, Vol. 1, No. 1, 2011, p. 74.

[114] Indrani Bagchi, "Iran Echoes India over Fillip to 'Opportunistic' Terrorism in Afghanistan," *Times of India*, January 2, 2013.

[115] "Baazieh Russiyeh ba Ghrab ba kart e Iran" ["Russia Using Iran Card in Game with West"], Jam-e Jam, January 7, 2010.

Iranian Constitutional Revolution, going so far as to surround and shell Iran's fledgling parliament, in order to preserve the reign of the pliant Qajar shah.

Following the First World War, the Soviet Union supported a separatist rebellion in Iran's northern region of Gilan. Again, at the end of the Second World War, the Soviets backed secessionist movements in Iranian Azerbaijan and Kurdistan. In 1946, Iran's Azerbaijan region became the site of one of the first U.S.-Soviet standoffs, brought on by Stalin's refusal to withdraw from Iranian territory. This event marked the beginning of Iran's integral role in the U.S. strategy to counter the USSR's influence in the Middle East. Despite its close alliance with the United States, however, the shah's government maintained "cordial, if not friendly," relations with the Soviets during most of the Cold War.[116]

The Iranian Revolution heralded an era of outward hostility toward the Soviet Union.[117] Referring to the atheist Soviet Union as the "Lesser Satan," Ayatollah Khomeini pursued a foreign policy that sought alliances with "neither East nor West." For their part, the Soviets backed the leftist Tudeh Party during the Islamic Republic's early power struggles, and strongly supported Saddam Hussein during the Iran-Iraq War.

The end of the Cold War coincided with a thaw in Russo-Iranian tensions.[118] With the fall of the Soviet Union, Khomeini's death, and the end of the Iran-Iraq War, Iran's leaders saw an opportunity to end hostilities. They also deemed improved relations with Moscow to be an important means of offsetting U.S. power in the region and of acquiring advanced weapons systems, which Russia was eager to sell. In the 1990s, Russia and Iran also began to cooperate in countering Sunni extremism in the region. The dissolution of the Soviet Union had resulted in independence movements and insurgencies among Russia's large Sunni minority. Like the Iranians, the Russians feared a Taliban victory in the Afghanistan civil war, concerned that the Taliban's support of extremist groups operating in the Central Asian republics would spill over across their borders.[119] In 1997, Iran played an instrumental role in diplomatically resolving a vicious civil war in Tajikistan between Islamist groups and the ruling ex-communists.[120] Iran also eased Russian concerns by not backing Islamist insurgents in Chechnya.[121] Moreover, in the Caucasus, Iran and Russia's shared interests in preventing Turkish and U.S. dominance brought them to side with Armenia in its conflict with the Western-backed Azerbaijan over Nagorno-Karabakh.[122]

Current Economic and Diplomatic Relations

Today, relations between Iran and Russia can be characterized as pragmatic but not one of absolute accommodation—what one Russian analyst has termed a "dialogue without

---

[116] Mark N. Katz, "Russian-Iranian Relations in the Putin Era," *Demokratizatsiya*, Vol. 10, No. 1, 2002, p. 69.

[117] Mark N. Katz, "Iran and Russia," in *The Iran Primer: Power, Politics, and U.S. Policy*, ed. Robin Wright, Washington, D.C.: United States Institute of Peace, 2010.

[118] Ibid.

[119] Mark N. Katz, "Russia, Iran, and Central Asia: Impact of the U.S. Withdrawal from Afghanistan," *Iran Regional Forum*, No. 13, September 2013.

[120] Ibid.

[121] Elaheh Koolaee, "Iran and Russia," paper presented at the Conference on Russia and Islam, Edinburgh, June 19–20, 2008.

[122] Katz, 2002.

commitments."[123] Russo-Iranian relations are a function of broader world events, reflecting convenient confluences of interest rather than affection and affinity. This is in part due to a lack of overall strategy in the way Russia deals with Iran, operating instead on a case-by-case basis.[124] As a result, relations can be friendly or tense depending on the issue at hand. This makes Moscow's policies toward Iran unpredictable and renders a strategic partnership unlikely.[125] According to Nikolay Kozhanov, a former attaché to the Russian embassy in Tehran, in the past two decades, it "is difficult to find another country whose relations with Moscow have experienced so many drastic twists in such a relatively short period."[126]

Despite the lack of a consistent approach, Russia's rivalry with the United States shapes its overall relations with Iran. Moscow views a U.S.-Iran rapprochement "as a serious threat to its interests in the region."[127] In fact, Russia's improvement of ties with Iran in the early 2000s may have been a direct response to Khatami's attempts to reach out to the United States.[128] In 2001, Khatami was invited to Moscow, where he signed the Treaty on the Basic Principles of Cooperation, which is still considered a "cornerstone" of Russia-Iran relations.[129] Russia also uses its relations with Tehran as a means of pressuring Washington. Therefore, periods of improvement in U.S.-Russia ties have generally coincided with cooling relations between Moscow and Tehran. For instance, when Russian President Vladimir Putin supported the George W. Bush administration's war on terror following the September 11, 2001, attacks, it caused a rift between the Islamic Republic and Russia.[130]

However, by 2006—a period coinciding with a rise in U.S.-Russia tensions—Russia and Iran had begun cooperating over energy issues.[131] And in 2007, Putin became the first Russian leader to visit Tehran since Stalin attended the Tehran Conference in 1943.[132] Bilateral relations again took a downward turn in 2009, following the Barack Obama administration's efforts to reset relations with Russia. In response to American overtures, President Dmitry Medvedev agreed to support further UN Security Council resolutions against Iran, and halted exports of the S-300 missile system to Iran the following year.[133] In response to the stalled S-300 deal, Tehran filed a $4 billion damage claim against Moscow at the international arbitration tribunal in Geneva.[134] That Russia bases its Iran relations on its strategy regarding the United States

---

[123] Nikolay Kozhanov, *Russia's Relations with Iran: Dialogue Without Commitments*, Policy Focus 120, Washington, D.C.: Washington Institute for Near East Policy, 2012.

[124] Ibid.

[125] Ibid.

[126] Ibid., p. 2.

[127] Ibid., p. 17.

[128] Ibid.

[129] Ibid., p. 6.

[130] Katz, 2002.

[131] Kozhanov, 2012.

[132] Nazila Fathi and C. J. Chivers, "In Iran, Putin Warns Against Military Action," *The New York Times*, October 17, 2007.

[133] Kozhanov, 2012.

[134] M. K. Bhadrakumar, "Russia and Iran: A Postmodern Dance," *Asia Times Online*, July 16, 2013.

is not lost on Iranian officials. Rouhani, for one, has warned that using "the Iran card in its game with the West, and particularly the U.S., has always been beneficial for Russia."[135]

Russia's involvement in the Iranian nuclear issue is representative of its double game with Iran and the West. While Russia would prefer that the Islamic Republic not develop a nuclear weapon capability, it also does not want to be seen as capitulating to U.S. demands. Furthermore, Russia is less concerned about Iran's nuclear program than the United States is, and is wary of overly pressuring Iran because of its need for Tehran's cooperation on economic and regional issues.[136]

Therefore, Moscow refrains from overtly supporting either side of the dispute. Russia's construction of the Bushehr nuclear reactor—long a source of tension between Tehran and Moscow—provides a case in point.[137] While Iran and Russia originally signed the deal in 1995 with a projected completion date of 1999, the reactor only reached full capacity in August 2012.[138] Iranian officials suspect that Russian construction delays were intended as a means of gaining concessions from the West.[139] Meanwhile, Russia at times has attempted to play a mediating role between Iran and the West. Officials in Moscow were reportedly angered by Tehran's repeated rejection of their offers from 2005 to 2009 to enrich uranium on Iran's behalf.[140]

Another source of Iranian wariness of Russia stems from the perception that Russia benefits from the Islamic Republic's economic isolation. Russian businesses operating in Iran appreciate the lack of competition from Western firms that have stayed away due to sanctions.[141] According to the analyst Meir Javedanfar, "As long as Iran remains a pariah state, Moscow can use Iran's isolation to sell them their outdated jets and secondhand products, which other countries would not buy from them."[142] In this regard, the Russian arms-export agency Rosoboronexport lobbies Moscow for close relations with Iran.[143] Trade is heavily balanced in Russia's favor; in 2010, Iranian exports to Russia totaled only $272 million, while Iran imported $3.4 billion in Russian goods.[144] Russia is also involved in infrastructure projects in Iran, including in the telecommunications and railroad industries.[145]

Energy issues pose yet another area of potential friction between Tehran and Moscow. As major exporters of energy products, Iran and Russia compete over both resources and market share. Ownership over resources in the Caspian Sea has been a particular source of contention

---

[135] Ibid.

[136] Katz, 2010.

[137] Ahmad Majidyar, "Russo-Iranian Relations from Iran's Perspective," Iran Tracker, May 20, 2009.

[138] Ibid.; "Rosatom Ready to Hand Bushehr Nuclear Plant to Iran," Radio Free Europe, August 9, 2013.

[139] Majidyar, 2009.

[140] Kozhanov, 2012.

[141] Ibid.

[142] Meir Javedanfar, "Russia Must Reassess Its Iran Policy," Real Clear World, August 17, 2009.

[143] Suggesting a correlation between Tehran's increasing isolation and its economic reliance on Moscow, Russian exports to Iran jumped from $864 million in 2006 to $3.8 billion in 2011. Katz, 2010; Kozhanov, 2012.

[144] Russia exports mostly ferrous metal and metallurgical products to Iran, while Iran exports mainly food and agricultural products to Russia. Kozhanov, 2012.

[145] Ibid.

between the two countries. Iran has pushed for Caspian rights to be divided equally among the five states lining its shores.[146] Russia, on the other hand, advocates allocating resources based on the amount of shoreline each country holds, which would leave Iran with only 13 percent of the resources.[147] Despite this competition, however, Russian energy companies have been active, since 2007, in Iranian energy development projects.[148] Part of Moscow's strategy in this regard appears to be focusing Iranian development in a manner that would not compete with Russia, for instance by directing Iranian LNG exports to East Asia rather than the European market.[149] Russia's expressed interest in assisting with the construction of the Iran-Pakistan pipeline may be part of this strategy.[150] It also may be an attempt by Moscow to pressure Washington.[151]

On security issues, Russia and Iran have many shared interests. While supportive of the U.S. and ISAF withdrawal from Afghanistan, the two countries fear a possible resurgence of Sunni extremist groups that would destabilize the region. Iranian-Russian collaboration in Afghanistan will likely improve bilateral relations, although Moscow will continue to view Iran as a junior and compliant partner in any joint endeavor. Karzai's visit to Russia in January 2011—the first visit by an Afghan president since 1991—indicated Moscow's intention to become increasingly involved in the country's affairs.[152] For instance, Russia is providing training and military equipment to Afghan soldiers and security forces.[153] It has trained 250 Afghan police officers, and in 2010 donated 20,000 AK-47s.[154] Russia announced in March 2013 that it was considering establishing military bases in Afghanistan that would serve to repair military hardware.[155]

Iran and Russia also are interested in maintaining the authoritarian status quo in the region, and are concerned about U.S. democratization efforts.[156] Highlighting this sentiment, in January 2007, Khamenei told Russian officials visiting Tehran that the "alliance between the Islamic Republic and the Russian Federation can stop U.S. ambitions to conquer the region."[157] When Ahmadinejad won a controversial reelection in 2009, Russia was the first country to host him, signaling Moscow's lack of interest in political change within Iran.[158]

Yet Iran's and Russia's mutual suspicion means that they remain "mired in a marriage of unembellished convenience" rather than a strategic alliance.[159] Even in instances where Tehran

---

[146] Katz, 2002.

[147] Ibid.

[148] Kozhanov, 2012.

[149] Sanati, 2013.

[150] Ibid.

[151] Ibid.

[152] Richard Weitz, "Russia's 'Return' to Afghanistan," *World Politics Review*, January 25, 2011.

[153] Ibid.

[154] Ibid.

[155] "Russia May Set Up New Afghanistan Bases: Official," RT, March 28, 2013.

[156] Katz, 2013.

[157] Majidyar, 2009.

[158] Javedanfar, 2009.

[159] Cory Bender, "Why Russia Won't Budge on Iran," *U.S. News and World Report*, October 30, 2012.

and Moscow share a common interest, such as protecting the Assad regime in Syria, they appear to pursue parallel, rather than coordinated, policies.[160] And though Russia sees Iran as an important regional player, it is also wary of an overly powerful Islamic Republic.[161] Therefore, Russia strives to funnel Iranian participation on regional issues through multilateral organizations such as the Shanghai Cooperation Organisation (SCO)—an institution heavily influenced by Russia and one in which Iran has only observer status.[162] This extends to Russia's collaboration with Iran in Afghanistan; there, Russia operates through a mix of the SCO, the Commonwealth of Independent States, and the Collective Security Treaty Organization.[163]

Future Trends

Overall, Iran-Russia ties are likely to remain complicated. In the near term, bilateral cooperation most probably will increase as tensions remain high between Moscow and Washington. With Putin back at the helm in the Kremlin, Russia is attempting to mend some of the rifts with Iran that arose during the Medvedev years. For instance, in July 2013, Iran and Russia held a joint naval drill in the Caspian Sea.[164] In the same month, it was reported that Putin was considering selling Iran its Antey-2500 air defense system as an alternative to the S-300.[165] Tehran and Moscow have also been brought closer together through their close support of Syrian President Bashar al-Assad against Western-backed rebel forces. Both Putin and Rouhani were outspoken critics of Obama's threat to strike the Assad regime following its use of chemical weapons against civilians in August 2013.[166]

Concern over the situation in postwithdrawal Afghanistan will also push the two countries to cooperate, especially amid fears of the recently growing strength of Central Asian jihadists based in northern Afghanistan.[167] Fighting drug trafficking will be an important joint effort in this regard, as narcotics sales provide a substantial source of revenue for extremist groups in the region.[168] Of further concern to Moscow is the poorly controlled Tajik-Afghan border, which allows drug traffickers to pass through to Kazakhstan and, ultimately, on to Russia.[169]

In the long term, however, Iran-Russia tensions appear inevitable, possibly limiting Russian-Iranian cooperation in other areas. Russia would not ultimately benefit from a powerful Iran, free from the grip of Western sanctions. While Moscow has thus far decided to cooperate with Tehran on energy issues in order to influence the direction Iran pursues, decreased Iranian isolation could change Russia's perceptions. Although economic cooperation has

---

[160] Dmitri Shlapentokh, "A View from Russia: Moscow and Tehran's Complex Relationship," *Iran Regional Forum*, No. 4, June, 2013.

[161] Kozhanov, 2012.

[162] Ibid.

[163] Ibid.

[164] Bhadrakumar, 2013.

[165] Ibid.

[166] "Rouhani, Putin Vow Greater Efforts to Prevent Syria Attack," Press TV, August 28, 2013.

[167] Saule Mukhametrakhimova, "Afghan Pullout Risks Central Asia Security," *Asia Times Online*, August 22, 2013.

[168] Ibid.

[169] Ibid.

improved in recent years, it is still relatively "underdeveloped," with active talks about projects masking the lack of progress on the implementation side.[170] A potential harbinger of future bilateral tensions, Russia's Gazprom agreed in 2011 to support construction of the Turkmenistan-Afghanistan-Pakistan-India (TAPI) pipeline, which the United States has touted as an alternative to the Iran-Pakistan pipeline.[171] Russia has also offered to enlarge the transport corridor to Afghanistan in order to help Western supplies reach Afghanistan after the 2016 troop withdrawal.[172]

Moreover, Russia's powerful business lobby is highly reliant on Western financing and technology, providing the United States with leverage to mitigate closer Iran-Russia economic ties.[173] The United States may also be able to gain Russia's cooperation through increased exchange of detailed information on Iran's nuclear program.[174] Refraining from deploying antimissile systems to Eastern Europe also would decrease Russia's threat perception and could result in Moscow's increased collaboration. The latter would be in line with Obama's February 2009 letter to Medvedev regarding the issue.[175]

The China Factor

China may not be one of the major actors in Afghanistan, but it does maintain significant influence. China, which maintains a 50-mile border with Afghanistan, has activities in the country that also impact Iran's Afghanistan strategy, namely by way of Beijing's influence on the behavior of other actors discussed in this chapter. China's main focus in Afghanistan, thus far, has been to protect its investments and personnel. As of 2012, China provided only $250 million in development aid to Afghanistan, while Japan had spent over $4 billion on reconstruction projects.[176] On the other hand, China has invested a great deal in Afghanistan's natural resources. In October 2012, a Chinese firm began extracting oil from the Amu Darya basin in Afghanistan.[177] China also has invested $3.5 billion in the Aynak copper mine.[178]

India's foreign policy strategy is greatly impacted by China, as the two growing economies compete for natural resources and Beijing maintains close ties with Islamabad.[179] Part of India's frustration with U.S. sanctions has been over the fact that, while Indian firms have lessened their presence in the Iranian market, Chinese companies have moved in to replace

---

[170] Kozhanov, 2012, p. 23.

[171] Weitz, 2011.

[172] "Russia May Set Up New Afghanistan Bases," 2013.

[173] Shlapentokh, 2013.

[174] Kozhanov, 2012.

[175] Majidyar, 2009.

[176] Jeffrey Hornung, "Why China Should Do More in Afghanistan," *The Diplomat*, August 1, 2012.

[177] "The New Great Game," 2013.

[178] Shiza Shahid, *Engaging Regional Players in Afghanistan: Threats and Opportunities*, Washington, D.C.: Center for Strategic and International Studies, 2009.

[179] Melanie Hanif, "Indian Involvement in Afghanistan in the Context of the South Asian Security System," *Journal of Strategic Security*, Vol. 3, No. 2, 2010.

them.[180] In fact, some analysts argue that India's decision to fund the Chabahar port expansion in Iran was driven by Pakistan's February 2013 decision to allow China to operate the Gwadar Port.[181]

Whereas Russia sees the United States as its main rival in the Middle East and Caucasus, its moves in Central Asia are largely influenced by its desire to balance against China. According to Ahmed Rashid, in recent years "China has broken the economic connections that traditionally tied Central Asia to Russia" and has emerged as the dominant regional power.[182] While in 2002, China's trade with Central Asia stood at only $1 billion, it had reached $28 billion by 2010.[183] On the other hand, Russian trade with Central Asian countries in 2010 was only $15 billion.[184] China has also edged out Russia in the Iranian market. While Russia had hoped that Iran would become more reliant on it as a result of international isolation, Russia has instead watched Chinese goods flood the Iranian market.[185] Sino-Iranian trade reached $30 billion in 2010, while Iran-Russia trade stood at less than $4 billion that year.[186]

Whether Beijing decides to play a more active role in postwithdrawal Afghanistan's security remains to be seen. However, according to Rashid, "Only China will have the economic strength and political goodwill to make peace, as well as the resources to fill the coming power vacuum," in 2016.[187]

In conclusion, India, Russia, and Iran have convergent interests in Afghanistan, which could lead to greater cooperation in the future. Iran also enjoys close political and economic ties with India and Russia beyond Afghanistan. A desire to prevent the Taliban from becoming more powerful can revitalize the informal coalition that backed the Northern Alliance in the 1990s. Cooperation in Afghanistan between the three powers can also help Iran lessen its isolation and ameliorate the effects of some sanctions. However, the United States should view Iran's cooperation with India and Russia in Afghanistan as a net positive. For example, joint economic ventures between Iran and India in Afghanistan have the potential to further stabilize Afghanistan by tying it to Central Asia markets, and making it less dependent on Pakistan.

Of all major regional players in Afghanistan, Iran and Pakistan have the most divergent interests. Pakistan is known to back the Taliban and other extremist Sunni Afghan groups; Islamabad is also likely to try to exert more influence in Afghanistan after the U.S. drawdown. At the same time, Pakistan's rivalry with Iran is tempered by growing economic and energy cooperation. While the United States may view Iran as a counterbalance to Pakistan, it should also be aware that the Iranian-Pakistani relationship is nuanced and not shaped by regional competition alone.

---

[180] Pant, 2011.

[181] Atul Aneja, "India to Develop Iranian Port," *The Hindu*, May 5, 2013.

[182] Ahmed Rashid, "Why, and What, You Should Know About Central Asia," *New York Review of Books*, August 15, 2013.

[183] Ibid.

[184] Ibid.

[185] Bender, 2012.

[186] Ibid.; Kozhanov, 2012.

[187] Rashid, 2013.

CHAPTER FOUR

Conclusion and Implications for the United States

Iranian influence in Afghanistan following the drawdown of international forces need not necessarily be a cause of concern for the United States. Although Tehran will use its cultural, political, and economic sway in an attempt to shape a post-2016 Afghanistan, Iran and the United States share core interests there: to prevent the country from again becoming dominated by the Taliban and a safe haven for al Qaeda.

Because maintaining stability and furthering development are the most effective means of arriving at that end state, these areas provide ripe opportunities for cooperation between the United States and Iran. Referring to U.S.-Iran relations in January 2014, President Rouhani commented: "Cooperating on issues of mutual interest and concern would contribute to easing tensions in our region as well."[1] At the same time, a peaceful resolution to the Iranian nuclear crisis and the continued strengthening of relative pragmatists in the Tehran government could lead to cooperation between Iran and the United States in Afghanistan.

To promote stability, the United States should attempt to cooperate with Iran in countering narcotics in Afghanistan and encourage efforts to bring Tehran and Kabul to an agreement over water sharing. While many of the disagreements between the two countries appear intractable and beholden to political interests in Tehran and Washington, combating drug trafficking and addressing water-usage issues would be relatively uncontroversial and nonpolitical. It could also lead to increased mutual trust that would benefit broader U.S.-Iran relations. To this end, the United States could lend logistical or financial support to the UN-facilitated Triangular Initiative, which fosters coordination among Iran, Pakistan, and Afghanistan in countering the drug trade. With regard to the Iran-Afghan water dispute, the United States should become active—through the UN and development organizations—in facilitating a mutually agreed upon water-usage system.[2]

It is important to note, however, that even if U.S.-Iran tensions remain, Iran's activities in Afghanistan are unlikely to run counter to overall U.S. objectives; Washington need not concern itself with the activities of regional actors in Afghanistan as long as they align with the United States' ultimate objective there.

Iran exercises considerable power in Afghanistan today. The two countries are tied together through shared language, culture, and religion. Dari, a dialect of Iran's official language, Persian, is widely spoken in Afghanistan. Up to 20 percent of Afghans, mostly the

---

[1]   Hassan Rouhani, "What Iran Wants in 2014," *Project Syndicate*, January 8, 2014.

[2]   Fatemeh Aman and Barbara Slavin, *Iran, Afghanistan, and South Asia: Resolving Regional Sources of Instability*, Washington, D.C.: Atlantic Council, 2013.

Hazara population, practice Shia Islam; some of them view Iran as their natural religious and political protector.

Iran is also an important economic actor in Afghanistan. It has provided Kabul up to $500 million for economic reconstruction and is one of Afghanistan's largest trading partners and investors. Iranian economic activity, which has included partnering with other powers, such as India, for development projects, has been largely positive for Afghan stability. Iran can also exercise significant political influence not just with Tajik- and Hazara-dominated political groups but with the central government in Kabul as well.

Iran has used its economic and ideological influence in order to (unsuccessfully) sabotage U.S.-Afghan cooperation. The Islamic Republic has also provided measured support to insurgents fighting U.S. and allied forces in Afghanistan. Iran is currently the only major power that opposes the BSA deal being negotiated between Washington and Kabul. Tehran fears that the United States will use Afghanistan as a base to undermine the Islamic Republic by supporting anti-Iranian insurgents, as well as carry out sabotage and espionage operations against Iran's nuclear facilities.

However, Iran may have several reasons to curtail or even stop its support to anti-American insurgents, and even support the BSA under the right conditions. The departure of most American forces may assuage Iranian anxiety, as Tehran will no longer have to contend with a sizable and potentially hostile military force on its doorstep. A peaceful resolution to the nuclear issue and reduced tensions between Iran and the United States are likely to reduce Iranian incentives for aiding Taliban elements.

And while the Revolutionary Guards appear to be behind the arming of insurgents, more-moderate figures such as Rouhani and the Iranian foreign minister Mohammad Javad Zarif are likely to oppose such tactics and instead advocate a more diplomatic approach, including consultation and cooperation with other powers, even including the United States. After all, it was Zarif who convinced the Tajik-dominated Northern Alliance to support Karzai as Afghanistan's new leader in 2002.

Iran's relations with Pakistan, India, and Russia will also impact the extent to which the Islamic Republic contributes to the future stability and development of Afghanistan. Overall U.S. interests in Afghanistan align not only with Iran's but also with India's and Russia's. Therefore, cooperation between Tehran, New Delhi, and Moscow in Afghanistan could serve U.S. interests as well.

Because Afghanistan will remain a central part of Pakistan's strategy of balancing against India, Islamabad is likely to expend a great deal of resources on dominating Afghanistan. More than any other regional power, Pakistan presents a challenge to Iranian interests in Afghanistan. But despite their differing positions on the ideal makeup of a future Kabul administration (Islamabad prefers the reintegration of former Taliban officials), Iran and Pakistan do share interests in stemming refugee flows and countering their respective Baluchi insurgencies—both of which would be exacerbated in the event of increased unrest in Afghanistan.

If, however, the security situation in Afghanistan were to deteriorate significantly, Iran and Pakistan would likely fall back to supporting the country's Shia and Sunni militant groups, respectively. The increased sectarianism likely to result from a resumed Afghan civil war would not serve U.S. interests, as it could further fan the flames of sectarian conflicts raging in other parts of the Muslim world. Furthermore, the current symbiotic economic relationship between the two countries could serve as an incentive for avoiding confrontation in Afghanistan. Therefore, Washington should encourage joint Iranian-Pakistani projects if a final nuclear deal with Iran is reached; U.S. attempts to disrupt energy cooperation between the two—for instance, the IPI pipeline—could be counterproductive.

In the long term, the extent to which Iran and Pakistan will maintain the current level of cordiality in their relations remains uncertain. The continued improvement of Iran-India relations will likely concern Pakistan. And in the event that a less isolated Iran emerges from the nuclear negotiations, officials in Tehran could feel more emboldened to criticize Islamabad over the plight of Pakistani Shias or the presence of anti-Iran insurgents in Pakistan's Baluchistan province.

Close Iran-India relations also serve to ensure long-term stability in Afghanistan. Indian infrastructure development projects could play an integral role in creating a stable and economically viable Afghanistan. Increased Indian economic involvement in Central Asia could also have the added benefit of balancing against Chinese activities in the region. However, for Afghanistan to remain a lucrative market for Indian investors, India must have viable access to the country as well as to the broader Central Asian market.

Thus, Iran's role would be an essential component of future Indian development efforts. Though in the overall bilateral relationship it appears that Iran needs India more than the other way around, both countries stand to benefit from each other's successes in Afghanistan. And so does the United States. Increased Iran-India collaboration could run the risk of disturbing officials in Pakistan. Pakistan's desire, however, to confront Iran in Afghanistan would likely be dampened if Pakistan were cooperating with the Iranians on broader economic issues.

Russia-Iran relations will have less of an impact on postwithdrawal Afghanistan's future than Iran's relations with Pakistan and India. While Moscow and Tehran share the same overall objectives—countering Sunni extremism and drug trafficking—Iran and Russia do not need each other's cooperation in order to pursue their interests in Afghanistan. For instance, as opposed to India, Russia does not require Iranian partnership to access Afghanistan or the other Central Asian markets. Moreover, Russia sees Iran as a junior partner and will likely interact with it most often through broader institutions such as the SCO, the Commonwealth of Independent States, and the Collective Security Treaty Organization. Regarding joint development projects with Iran and India, Russia will assist insofar as they are lucrative for Russian businesses.

While Russia would prefer not to see a U.S.-Iran rapprochement, such an outcome would not undermine its limited cooperation with Iran in Afghanistan. A risk factor, however, is Russia's intended involvement in the U.S.-backed construction of the TAPI pipeline, which is being touted as an alternative to the proposed IPI pipeline. Continued U.S. obstruction of the IPI project could increase Iran's incentive to sabotage the construction and operation of the TAPI pipeline.

Shared interests between India, Russia, and Iran in Afghanistan should make Washington consider Iran an important regional actor in stabilizing Afghanistan. Thus, it is worthwhile to include Iran in regional and international discussions on Afghan security, especially if Iran comes to accept any residual international force in Afghanistan.

If, following the drawdown of international forces, the ANSF fails to successfully continue its fight against terrorism, Iran is well situated to support Tajik and Hazara groups that could again fight a resurgent Taliban.

The dispute over Iran's nuclear program has intensified U.S.-Iran tensions. Iran's influence in Afghanistan, however, should not be viewed in zero-sum terms. Iran and the United

States have convergent interests there. It is therefore prudent that the United States engage the Iranian government in bilateral discussions regarding Afghanistan and pursue joint activities that would serve their mutual interests and build much-needed trust.

References

Abbas, Hassan, *Pakistan's Drift into Extremism: Allah, the Army, and America's War on Terror*, Armonk, N.Y.: M.E. Sharpe, 2005.

Abbasi, Abrahim, and Majid Ranjbardar, "Komak-haye Mali-e Iran be Afghanistan: Ahdaf va Asar-e Eqtesadi-ye an" ["Financial Assistance to Afghanistan: Goals and Economic Effects of It"], *Foreign Relations Quarterly*, Vol. 3, Fall 1990.

"Afghan Refugees in Iran & Pakistan," European Resettlement Network. As of November 6, 2013: http://www.resettlement.eu/page/afghan-refugees-iran-pakistan-0

"Afghan Refugees Pin Their Hopes on Rouhani," Deutsche Welle, July 31, 2013. As of November 6, 2013: http://www.dw.de/afghan-refugees-pin-their-hopes-on-rouhani/a-16989349

"Afghans Demonstrate Against Iranian 'Ill-Treatment,'" BBC News, May 6, 2010. As of April 21, 2014: http://news.bbc.co.uk/2/hi/8664289.stm

Afrasiabi, Kaveh L., "The Iran-Pakistan Nexus," *Asia Times Online*, January 13, 2006. As of November 7, 2013: http://www.atimes.com/atimes/South_Asia/HA13Df03.html

Alam, Shah, "The Changing Paradigm of Iranian Foreign Policy Under Khatami," *Strategic Analysis*, Vol. 24, No. 9, December 2000, pp. 1629–1653.

Aman, Fatemeh, "Afghan Water Infrastructure Threatens Iran, Regional Stability," *Al-Monitor*, January 7, 2013. As of November 6, 2013: http://www.al-monitor.com/pulse/originals/2013/01/afghanwatershortageiranpakistan.html

Aman, Fatemeh, and Barbara Slavin, *Iran, Afghanistan, and South Asia: Resolving Regional Sources of Instability*, Washington, D.C.: Atlantic Council, 2013.

Ameli, Saied Reza, and Hamideh Molaei, "Religious Affiliation and Intercultural Sensitivity: Interculturality Between Shia and Sunni Muslims in Iran," *International Journal of Intercultural Relations*, Vol. 36, No. 1, 2012, pp. 31–40.

Amnesty International, *Iran: Human Rights Abuses Against the Baluchi Minority*, September 2007. As of April 18, 2014: http://www.amnesty.org/en/library/asset/MDE13/104/2007/en/1463de4f-d370-11dd-a329-2f46302a8cc6/mde131042007en.pdf

Aneja, Atul, "India to Develop Iranian Port," *The Hindu*, May 5, 2013. As of November 7, 2013: http://www.thehindu.com/news/national/india-to-develop-iranian-port/article4684162.ece

Ansar, Arif, "Future of Pakistan-Iran Ties," *Pakistan Today*, January 27, 2013. As of November 7, 2013: http://www.pakistantoday.com.pk/2013/01/27/comment/columns/future-of-pakistan-iran-ties

Arnold, Tom, "Iran Looks to Pakistan for Food Deal," *The National*, April 23, 2012. As of November 7, 2013: http://www.thenational.ae/business/industry-insights/economics/iran-looks-to-pakistan-for-food-deal

"Baazieh Russiyeh ba Ghrab ba kart e Iran" ["Russia Using Iran Card in Game with West"], Jam-e Jam, January 7, 2010. As of November 7, 2013: http://www1.jamejamonline.ir/PaperText.aspx?newsnum=100864064235

Bagchi, Indrani. "India Votes Against Iran at IAEA," *Times of India*, November 28, 2009. As of November 7, 2013:
http://articles.timesofindia.indiatimes.com/2009-11-28/
india/28074607_1_india-votes-iaea-resolution-nuclear-programme

———, "Iran Echoes India over Fillip to 'Opportunistic' Terrorism in Afghanistan," *Times of India*, January 2, 2013. As of November 7, 2013:
http://articles.timesofindia.indiatimes.com/2013-01-02/
south-asia/36111207_1_jalili-afghanistan-s-high-peace-council-iran-s-parchin

Basar, Eray, *The Roles of India and Pakistan in Afghanistan's Development and Natural Resources*, ed. Steven A. Zyck, Norfolk, Va.: Civil-Military Fusion Centre, 2012.

Bender, Cory, "Why Russia Won't Budge on Iran," *U.S. News and World Report*, October 30, 2012. As of November 7, 2013:
http://www.usnews.com/opinion/blogs/world-report/2012/10/30/russia-united-states-divided-on-iran

Bhadrakumar, M. K., "Russia and Iran: A Postmodern Dance," *Asia Times Online*, July 16, 2013. As of November 7, 2013:
www.atimes.com/atimes/Central_Asia/CEN-01-260713.html

Bhattacharya, Prasenjit, "Iran Slips to 7th Among India's Oil Suppliers," *The Wall Street Journal*, March 15, 2013. As of November 7, 2013:
http://online.wsj.com/article/SB10001424127887324077704578361720153829386.html

Bokhari, Farhan, "Tensions Rise Between Pakistan and Iran," CBS News, October 19, 2009. As of November 7, 2013: http://www.cbsnews.com/stories/2009/10/19/world/main5395154.shtml

Bush, George W., "State of the Union Address," delivered at the U.S. Capitol, January 29, 2002.

Carter, Sarah A., "Iran Training Taliban Fighters to Use Surface to Air Missiles," *Washington Examiner*, October 24, 2010.

Chandrasekaran, A. V., "Afghanistan: India's Interests," *Defense and Diplomacy Journal*, Vol. 1, No. 1, 2011, p. 74.

Christensen, Janne Bjerre, *Strained Alliances: Iran's Troubled Relations to Afghanistan and Pakistan*, Copenhagen: Danish Institute for International Studies, 2011.

Crises Analysis Group Pakistan's Strategic Studies Center, "Bohran-e Afghanistan az chand Didgah" ["The Afghanistan Crisis from Various Viewpoints"], *Strategic Studies*, Vol. 11, No. 3, 1988.

Cronin, Richard, Alan Kronstadt, and Sharon Squassoni, *Pakistan's Nuclear Proliferation Activities and the Recommendations to the 9/11 Commission: I.S. Policy Constraints and Options*, Washington, D.C.: Congressional Research Service, 2010.

Dobbins, Jim, "Engaging Iran, United States Institute of Peace," *The Iran Primer*, United States Institute of Peace, October 22, 2013. As of April 18, 2014:
http://iranprimer.usip.org/resource/engaging-iran

Donati, Jessica, "Afghan President Karzai's Brother to Offer Him Role If Elected," Reuters, October 11, 2013. As of October 14, 2013:
http://news.yahoo.com/afghan-president-karzais-brothers-offer-him-role-elected-054856303--sector.html

Dunn, David Hastings, "Real Men Want to Go to Tehran: Bush, Pre-emption and the Iranian Nuclear Challenge," *International Affairs*, Vol. 83, No. 1, 2007, pp. 19–38.

Engel, Richard, and Robert Windrem, "Israel Teams with Terror Group to Kill Iran's Nuclear Scientists, U.S. Officials Tell NBC News," NBC News, February 9, 2012. As of April 18, 2014:
http://rockcenter.nbcnews.com/_news/2012/02/09/10354553-israel-teams-with-terror-group-to-kill-irans-nuclear-scientists-us-officials-tell-nbc-ne

Erdbrink, Thomas, "The West's Stalwart Ally in the War on Drugs: Iran (Yes, That Iran)," *The New York Times*, October 11, 2012. As of November 6, 2013:
http://mobile.nytimes.com/2012/10/12/world/middleeast/iran-fights-drug-smuggling-at-borders.html?pagewanted=all&_r=0

Escobar, Pepe, "All Aboard the New Silk Road(s)," Al Jazeera, September 16, 2012. As of November 7, 2013:
http://www.aljazeera.com/indepth/opinion/2012/09/20129138245360573.html

Fair, Christine C., "India and Iran: New Delhi's Balancing Act," *The Washington Quarterly*, Vol. 30, No. 3, Summer 2008, pp. 145–159.

Farhi, Farideh, "On Khamenei's Response to Obama," *Informed Comment: Global Affairs* (blog), March 22, 2009. As of April 18, 2014:
http://icga.blogspot.com/2009/03/on-khameneis-response-to-obama.html

Farmer, Ben, "Iran Threatens to Expel Afghan Refugees If Kabul Ratifies US Strategic Partnership," *The Telegraph*, May 10, 2012. As of:
http://www.telegraph.co.uk/news/worldnews/asia/afghanistan/9256602/Iran-threatens-to-expel-Afghan-refugees-if-Kabul-ratifies-US-strategic-partnership.html

Fathi, Nazila, and C. J. Chivers, "In Iran, Putin Warns Against Military Action," *The New York Times*, October 17, 2007. As of November 7, 2013:
http://www.nytimes.com/2007/10/17/world/middleeast/17iran.html?pagewanted=all&_r=0

Ferris-Rotman, Amie, "Iran Pushes Out Afghans as Regional Power-Play Heats Up," Reuters, December 2, 2012. As of November 6, 2013:
http://www.reuters.com/article/2012/12/02/us-afghanistan-iran-refugees-idUSBRE8B103T20121202

Filkins, Dexter, "Afghans Report Ethnic Massacre by Taliban," *Los Angeles Times*, September 18, 1998.

———, "Iran Is Said to Give Top Karzai Aide Cash by the Bagful," *The New York Times*, October 23, 2010.

Fineren, Daniel, "India Trumps Pakistan's Iran Rice Trade Boom with Oil Rupees," Reuters, March 8, 2013. As of November 7, 2013:
http://in.reuters.com/article/2013/03/08/india-iran-rice-idINDEE92703K20130308

Graham-Harrison, Emma, "Afghan Taliban Send Delegation to Iran," *The Guardian*, June 3, 2013. As of November 4, 2013:
http://www.theguardian.com/world/2013/jun/03/afghan-taliban-send-delegation-iran

Hadian, Nasser, "Nasser Hadian on Why Iran Is Ready," *The Iran Primer*, United States Institute of Peace, September 20, 2013. As of April 18, 2014:
http://iranprimer.usip.org/blog/2013/sep/20/nasser-hadian-why-iran-ready

"Hameh kesani ke be sepah esteham zadand" ["All the People Who Accused the Revolutionary Guards"], *Mehr News Magazine*, February 28, 2013. As of November 6, 2013:
http://webzine.mehrnews.com/FullStory/News/?NewsId=619

Hanif, Melanie, "Indian Involvement in Afghanistan in the Context of the South Asian Security System," *Journal of Strategic Security*, Vol. 3, No. 2, 2010, pp. 13–26.

Hornung, Jeffrey, "Why China Should Do More in Afghanistan," *The Diplomat*, August 1, 2012. As of November 7, 2013:
http://thediplomat.com/2012/08/01/why-china-should-do-more-in-afghanistan

Houk, Andrew, "Iran's Response to Drugs from Afghanistan," Stimson Center, January 28, 2011a. As of November 6, 2013:
http://www.stimson.org/spotlight/irans-response-to-drugs-from-afghanistan/

———, "Transboundary Water Sharing: Iran and Afghanistan," Stimson Center, March 22, 2011b. As of April 21, 2014:
http://www.stimson.org/spotlight/transboundary-water-sharing-iran-and-afghanistan/

Ibrahimi, Niamatullah, "The Failure of a Clerical Proto-State: Hazarajat, 1979–1984," working paper no. 6, Crisis States Research Center, London School of Economics and Political Science, September 2006.

———, "The Dissipation of Political Capital Among Afghanistan's Hazaras: 2001–2009," working paper no. 51, Crisis States Research Center, London School of Economics and Political Science, June 2009.

Imtiaz, Huma, "Iran Pipeline Deal: Pakistan Should Avoid 'Sanctionable Activity,' Says US," *Express Tribune*, February 28, 2012. As of November 7, 2013:
http://tribune.com.pk/story/513820/iran-pipeline-deal-pakistan-should-avoid-sanctionable-activity-says-us

"India Mulls Insurance Guarantee for Refiners Using Iran Oil," Reuters, August 8, 2013. As of November 7, 2013:
http://www.voanews.com/content/reu-mulls-insurance-guarantee-for-refiners-using-iran-oil/1726311.html

"India Sends Team to Iran over Tanker," Islamic Republic of Iran Broadcasting, August 20, 2013.

"India to Pay in Rupees for Iran's Oil," *Deccan Herald*, July 14, 2013. As of November 7, 2013:
http://www.deccanherald.com/content/344862/india-pay-rupees-iran039s-oil.htm

"Iran and Pakistan Sign 'Historic' Pipeline Deal," BBC News, March 17, 2010. As of November 7, 2013:
http://news.bbc.co.uk/2/hi/8572267.stm

"Iran Cancels Pakistan Gas Pipeline Loan," Associated Press, December 14, 2013. As of January 8, 2014:
http://abcnews.go.com/m/story?id=21218219

"Iran 'Expels' Afghan Warlord," BBC News, February 26, 2002. As of October 23, 2013:
http://news.bbc.co.uk/2/hi/middle_east/1842427.stm

"Iran Funds Gas Pipeline to Pakistan," Press TV, January 30 2013. As of November 7, 2013:
http://www.presstv.ir/detail/2013/01/30/286401/iran-funds-gas-pipeline-to-pakistan

"Iran Imports Vehicles, Medicines from India to Bypass US-Led Oil Sanctions," Iran's View, May 17, 2013. As of November 7, 2013:
http://www.iransview.com/iran-to-import-vehicles-medicines-from-india-to-bypass-us-led-oil-sanctions/653

"Iran Keen to Import Drugs from India," Fars News Agency, January 3, 2013. As of November 7, 2013:
http://www.payvand.com/news/13/jan/1025.html

"Iran on 'Frontline' of Fight Against Drug Smuggling," *Al Arabiya*, June 26, 2013. As of November 6, 2013:
http://english.alarabiya.net/en/variety/2013/06/26/Iran-on-frontline-of-fight-against-drug-smuggling-.html

"Iran-Pakistan Trade Rises Despite U.S. Sanctions," Press TV, March 17, 2012. As of November 7, 2013:
http://www.presstv.com/detail/232200.html

"Iran to Accept Wheat, Meat, Rice as Payment for Fuel," Reuters, February 21, 2013. As of November 7, 2013:
http://www.reuters.com/article/2013/02/21/iran-pakistan-refinery-idUSL6N0BL8I320130221

Javedanfar, Meir, "Russia Must Reassess Its Iran Policy," Real Clear World, August 17, 2009. As of November 7, 2013:
http://www.realclearworld.com/articles/2009/08/17/russia_must_reassess_its_iran_policy_97064.html

———, "Iran's New Opportunity to Improve Relations with Pakistan," Al-Monitor, May 28, 2012. As of November 7, 2013:
http://www.al-monitor.com/pulse/originals/2012/al-monitor/irans-pakistani-opportunity-in-a.html

Jawad, Nassim, *Afghanistan: A Nation of Minorities*, London: Minority Rights Group, 1992.

Jehl, Douglas, "Iran Holds Taliban Responsible for 9 Diplomats' Deaths," *The New York Times*, September 11, 1998.

Johnson, Thomas H., "Ismail Khan, Herat, and Iranian Influence," *Strategic Insights*, Vol. 3, No. 7, July 2004.

Jorisch, Avi, "Port of Damaged Goods: India's Dangerous Investment in Iran's Chabahar," *Forbes*, September 16, 2013.

Joshi, Yogesh, "As U.S. Leaves Afghanistan, India Reconsiders Iran Policy," *World Politics Review*, May 9, 2013. As of November 7, 2013:
http://www.worldpoliticsreview.com/articles/12931/as-u-s-leaves-afghanistan-india-reconsiders-iran-policy

"Jundullah Claims Responsibility for Terror Attack," Press TV, October 18, 2009. As of April 18, 2014:
http://edition.presstv.ir/detail/108982.html

Kagan, Frederick W., Kimberly Kagan, and Danielle Pletka, *Iranian Influence in the Levant, Iraq, and Afghanistan*, Washington, D.C.: American Enterprise Institute, 2008.

Karimi, Nasser, "Iran Releases Video Allegedly Captured by Crashed US Spy Drone," Associated Press, February 7, 2013.

Karthikeya, Raja, "India's Iran Calculus," *Foreign Policy*, September 24, 2010. As of November 7, 2013: http://mideast.foreignpolicy.com/posts/2010/09/24/indias_iran_calculus

Katz, Mark N.,"Russian-Iranian Relations in the Putin Era," *Demokratizatsiya*, Vol. 10, No. 1, 2002, p. 69–81.

———, "Iran and Russia," in *The Iran Primer: Power, Politics, and U.S. Policy*, ed. Robin Wright, 186–189. Washington, D.C.: United States Institute of Peace, 2010.

———, "Russia, Iran, and Central Asia: Impact of the U.S. Withdrawal from Afghanistan," *Iran Regional Forum*, No. 3, September 2013.

Khalilzad, Zalmay, "Afghanistan in 1994: Civil War and Disintegration," *Asian Survey*, Vol. 35, No. 2, February 1995, pp. 147–152.

Khan, M. Ilyas, "Formidable Power of Pakistan's Anti-Shia Militants," BBC News, January 11, 2013. As of November 7, 2013: http://www.bbc.co.uk/news/world-asia-20983153

"Khatami Speaks of Dialogue Among Civilizations," *Iranian Diplomacy*, October 2, 2010. As of April 18, 2014: http://www.irdiplomacy.ir/en/page/8798/Khatami+Speaks+of+Dialogue+among+Civilizations.html

Khoshkho, Jalil, "Sistan va Baluchestan: Faghr Dirinie va Hasasiyat haye Konuni" ["Sistan and Baluchestan: Long Existing Poverty and Today's Sensitivities"], *Gozaresh Political and Social*, Vol. 127, October 2001.

Koolaee, Elaheh, "Iran and Russia," paper presented at the Conference on Russia and Islam, Edinburgh, June 19–20, 2008. As of April 18, 2014: http://www.pol.ed.ac.uk/__data/assets/pdf_file/0004/28687/Iran_and_Russia.pdf

Kozhanov, Nikolay, *Russia's Relations with Iran: Dialogue Without Commitments*, Policy Focus 120, Washington, D.C.: Washington Institute for Near East Policy, 2012.

Looking at Iran: How 20 Arab and Muslim Nations View Iran and Its Policies, Washington, D.C.: Zogby Research Services, 2012.

"Majara-ye Didar-e Marja'e Shi'iyan-e Afghanistan ba Rahbar-e Enghelab" ["Afghanistan's Shia Marja Visits the Leader of the Revolution"], Shia-Online, May 6, 2013.

Majidyar, Ahmad, "Russo-Iranian Relations from Iran's Perspective," Iran Tracker, May 20, 2009. As of November 7, 2013: http://www.irantracker.org/analysis/russo-iranian-relations-irans-perspective

Majidyar, Ahmad, and Ali Alfoneh, "Iranian Influence in Afghanistan: Imam Khomeini Relief Committee," *Middle East Outlook*, Vol. 4, 2010.

Maley, William, *The Foreign Policy of the Taliban*, New York: Council on Foreign Relations Press, February 2000.

Malik, Hasan Yaser, "Strategic Importance of Gwadar Port," *Journal of Political Studies*, Vol. 19, No. 2, 2012, pp. 57–69.

Mallet, Victor, "Afghanistan's Forgotten Crisis: Its Economy," *Financial Times*, May 20, 2013. As of October 14, 2013: http://www.ft.com/cms/s/0/59d9a5ae-b21e-11e2-a388-00144feabdc0.html#axzz2hieB4AMo

Mehdudia, Sujay, "Sanctions Weigh on India as It Considers Iran's Gas Offer," *The Hindu*, July 14, 2013. As of November 7, 2013: http://www.thehindu.com/business/Industry/sanctions-weigh-on-india-as-it-considers-irans-gas-offer/article4914938.ece

Mikser, Sven, *Transition in Afghanistan: Assessing the Security Effort*, NATO Parliamentary Assembly, draft general report, April 8, 2011.

Milani, Mohsen M., "Iran's Policy Towards Afghanistan," *Middle East Journal*, Vol. 60, No. 2, Spring 2006, pp. 235–256.

————, "Iran's Ties to the Taliban," *The Iran Primer*, United States Institute of Peace, August 10, 2011. As of April 18, 2014:
http://iranprimer.usip.org/blog/2011/aug/10/iran%E2%80%99s-ties-taliban

Mohmand, Abdul-Qayum, *The Prospects for Economic Development in Afghanistan: Reflections on a Survey of the Afghan People*, Part 2 of 4, Washington, D.C.: Asia Foundation, 2012.

Mojde, Vahid, *Ravabat-e Siyasi-ye Iran va Afghanistan dar Qarn-e Bistom* [*Iran and Afghanistan's Political Relations in the 20th Century*], Maiwand, Afghanistan: Maiwand Publishing Company, 2010.

Mukhametrakhimova, Saule, "Afghan Pullout Risks Central Asia Security," *Asia Times Online*, August 22, 2013. As of November 7, 2013:
http://www.atimes.com/atimes/Central_Asia/CEN-01-220813.html

Nader, Alireza, "Ahmadinejad vs. the Revolutionary Guards," *The Iran Primer*, United States Institute of Peace, July 11, 2011. As of November 6, 2013:
http://iranprimer.usip.org/blog/2011/jul/11/ahmadinejad-vs-revolutionary-guards

Nader, Alireza, and Joya Laha, *Iran's Balancing Act in Afghanistan*, Santa Monica, Calif.: RAND Corporation, 2011.

Nasseri, Ladane, "Iran, Afghanistan Trade Hits $2 Billion in 2011, IRNA Reports," Bloomberg, December 25, 2011. As of April 21, 2014:
http://www.bloomberg.com/news/2011-12-25/iran-afghanistan-trade-hits-2-billion-in-2011-irna-reports.html

Nazar, Zarif, and Charles Recknagel, "Controversial Madrasah Builds Iran's Influence in Kabul," Radio Free Europe/Radio Liberty, November 6, 2010. As of April 28, 2014:
http://www.rferl.org/content/Controversial_Madrasah_Builds_Irans_Influence_In_Kabul/2212566.html

"The New Great Game," *The Economist*, Intelligence Unit, January 30, 2013. As of November 7, 2013:
http://country.eiu.com/article.aspx?articleid=1890101173&Country=Afghanistan&topic=Politics

Nicoletti, Michael, "Opium Production and Distribution: Poppies, Profits and Power in Afghanistan," thesis, DePaul University, 2011.

Nordland, Rod, "Production of Opium by Afghans Is up Again," *The New York Times*, April 15, 2013. As of November 6, 2013:
http://mobile.nytimes.com/2013/04/16/world/asia/afghanistan-opium-production-increases-for-3rd-year.html

Nouri, Elham, "Taghviyat e ravabat e Iran Va Hind" ["Strengthening of Iran-India Ties and Its Impact on Regional Development and Stability"], Center for Scientific Research and Middle East Strategic Studies, September 17, 2012. As of November 7, 2013:
http://fa.merc.ir/default.aspx?tabid=127&ArticleId=1756

"Pakistan Calls for More Trade with Iran," *Tehran Times*, November 20, 2012. As of November 7, 2013:
http://www.tehrantimes.com/economy-and-business/103467-pakistan-calls-for-more-trade-with-iran

Pant, Harsh V., "Pakistan and Iran's Dysfunctional Relationship," *Middle East Quarterly*, Vol. 16, Spring 2009, pp. 43–50.

————, "Delhi's Tehran Conundrum," *The Wall Street Journal*, September 20, 2010. As of November 7, 2013:
http://online.wsj.com/article/SB10001424052748703556604575502611786589130.html

————, "India's Relations with Iran: Much Ado About Nothing," *Washington Quarterly*, Vol. 34, No. 1, 2011, pp. 61–74.

"Pasokh Rouhani be payam tabrik enokhost vazir e Hind," ["Rouhani's Response to Messages of Congratulations from Prime Minister of India, Head of Indonesian Parliament, and President of Montenegro"], *Khabar Online*, July 8, 2013. As of November 7, 2013:
http://www.khabaronline.ir/detail/302598

Peters, Gretchen, *How Opium Profits the Taliban*, Washington, D.C.: United States Institute of Peace, 2009.

Peterson, Scott, "Why a Dam in Afghanistan Might Set Back Peace," *Christian Science Monitor*, July 30, 2013. As of November 7, 2013:
http://www.csmonitor.com/World/Asia-South-Central/2013/0730/
Why-a-dam-in-Afghanistan-might-set-back-peace

Pew Forum on Religion and Public Life, *Mapping the Global Muslim Population: A Report on the Size and Distribution of the World's Muslim Population*, Washington, D.C.: Pew Research Center, 2009.

"PM Congratulates Rouhani," *Business Standard*, July 21, 2013. As of November 7, 2013:
http://www.business-standard.com/article/pti-stories/pm-congratulates-rouhani-113061801151_1.html

Pouladi, Farhad, "More Iran-India Trade Would Boost Ties: Delegation," AFP, March 10, 2012. As of April 18, 2014:
https://au.finance.yahoo.com/news/more-iran-india-trade-boost-083702603.html

Prashad, Vijay, "The Iran-India-Afghanistan Riddle," *Asia Times Online*, August 28, 2012a. As of November 7, 2013:
http://www.atimes.com/atimes/Middle_East/NH28Ak02.html

———, "Silk Road Nears an Historic Opening," *Asia Times Online*, September 12, 2012b. As of November 7, 2013:
http://www.atimes.com/atimes/Middle_East/NI12Ak01.html

"Qayum Karzai: Omidvaram Baradaram dar Entekhabat Bitaraf Bemunad ["Qayum Karzai: I Hope My Brother Remains Neutral in the Elections"], Harun Najafizadeh's interview with Qayum Karzai, BBC Persian, October 14, 2013. As of October 28, 2013:
http://www.bbc.co.uk/persian/iran/2013/10/131014_l46_af_elex.shtml

"Rahbar Shi'ayan-e Afghanistan: Iran Olguye Monasebi baraye Keshvar haye Islami ast" ["Afghanistan's Shi'a Leader: Iran Is an Appropriate Role Model for Islamic Countries"], Iranian Students' News Agency, November 22, 2010.

Rashid, Ahmed, "Why, and What, You Should Know About Central Asia," *New York Review of Books*, August 15, 2013. As of November 7, 2013:
http://www.nybooks.com/articles/archives/2013/aug/15/why-and-what-you-should-know-about-central-asia

"Refugee Matters in Iran," Norwegian Refugee Council report, Vol. 1, No. 6, December 2012–January 2013. As of November 6, 2013:
http://www.nrc.no/arch/_img/9669332.pdf

"Report: Afghans Paid $3.9 Billion in Bribes Last Year," Afghanistan Study Group, February 11, 2013. As of April 18, 2014:
http://www.afghanistanstudygroup.org/2013/02/11/report-afghans-paid-3-9-billion-in-bribes-last-year/

Riedel, Bruce O., "The Clinton Administration," *The Iran Primer*, United States Institute of Peace. As of October 29, 2013:
http://iranprimer.usip.org/resource/clinton-administration

Risen, James, "Reports Link Karzai's Brother to Afghanistan Heroin Trade," *The New York Times*, October 4, 2008. As of November 6, 2013:
http://www.nytimes.com/2008/10/05/world/asia/05afghan.html?pagewanted=all&_r=0

Rivera, Ray, "Afghanistan Strained by Shortages as Iran Tightens Flow of Fuel," *The New York Times*, January 9, 2011.

"Rosatom Ready to Hand Bushehr Nuclear Plant to Iran," Radio Free Europe, August 9, 2013. As of November 7, 2013:
http://www.rferl.org/content/bushehr-russia-iran-nuclear-control/25070637.html

"Roshd-e Tashi'o dar Afghanistan va Naghsh-e Iran" ["The Growth of Shi'ism in Afghanistan and the Role of Iran"], BBC Persian, January 6, 2009.

Rouhani, Hassan, "What Iran Wants in 2014," Project Syndicate, January 8, 2014. As of January 9, 2014:
http://www.project-syndicate.org/commentary/hassan-rouhani-on-iran-s-new-moderation

"Rouhani, Putin Vow Greater Efforts to Prevent Syria Attack," Press TV, August 28, 2013. As of November 7, 2013:
http://www.presstv.com/detail/2013/08/28/320990/iran-russia-to-step-up-antiwar-effort

Roy, Meena Singh, "India and Iran Relations: Sustaining the Momentum," ISDA issue brief, Institute for Defense Studies and Analyses, 2013.

Rubenfeld, Samuel, "Treasury Sanctions Iranian General for Afghan Heroin Trafficking," *The Wall Street Journal*, March 7, 2012. As of November 6, 2013:
http://blogs.wsj.com/corruption-currents/2012/03/07/
treasury-sanctions-iranian-general-for-afghan-heroin-trafficking/

Rubinstein, Alvin Z., "The Soviet Union and Iran Under Khomeini," *International Affairs*, Vol. 57, No. 4, Autumn 1981, pp. 599–617.

"Russia May Set Up New Afghanistan Bases: Official," RT, March 28, 2013. As of November 7, 2013:
http://rt.com/politics/bases-official-afghanistan-return-985

Sadjadpour, Karim, *Reading Khamenei: The World View of Iran's Most Powerful Leader*, Washington, D.C.: Carnegie Endowment for International Peace, 2009.

Sahimi, Muhammad, "Iran Election Roundup: Television and Revelations," Muftah, May 27, 2013. As of November 7, 2013:
http://muftah.org/iran-election-roundup-television-and-revelations

Samii, Bill, "Iran/Afghanistan: Still No Resolution for Century-Old Water Dispute," Radio Free Europe/Radio Liberty, September 7, 2005. As of November 6, 2013:
http://www.rferl.org/content/article/1061209.html

Sanati, Reza, "Pipeline Politics," *Cairo Review of Global Affairs*, July 21, 2013. As of November 7, 2013:
http://www.aucegypt.edu/GAPP/CairoReview/Pages/articleDetails.aspx?aid=386

Sedghi, Ami, "UNHCR 2012 Refugee Statistics: Full Data," *The Guardian*, June 19, 2013. As of November 6, 2013:
http://www.guardian.co.uk/news/datablog/2013/jun/19/refugees-unhcr-statistics-data

Seibert, Thomas, "Afghan Refugees Leave Iran for Turkey," *The National*, February 17, 2013. As of November 7, 2013:
http://www.thenational.ae/news/world/europe/afghan-refugees-leave-iran-for-turkey

Shahid, Shiza, *Engaging Regional Players in Afghanistan: Threats and Opportunities*, Washington, D.C.: Center for Strategic and International Studies, 2009.

Shelala, Robert M., II, Nori Kasting, and Anthony H. Cordesman, *U.S. and Iranian Strategic Competition: Afghanistan, Pakistan, India, and Central Asia*, working draft, Washington, D.C.: Center for Strategic and International Studies, 2012.

Shlapentokh, Dmitri, "A View from Russia: Moscow and Tehran's Complex Relationship," *Iran Regional Forum*, No. 4, June 2013.

Solomon, Jay, and Subhadip Sircar, "India Joins U.S. Effort to Stifle Iran Trade," *The Wall Street Journal*, December 29, 2010. As of November 7, 2013:
http://online.wsj.com/article/SB10001424052970203513204576046893652486616.html

Squassoni, Sharon, "Closing Pandora's Box: Pakistan's Role in Nuclear Proliferation," *Arms Control Today*, April 2004. As of November 7, 2013:
http://www.armscontrol.org/act/2004_04/Squassoni#notes20

Strand, Arne, Astri Suhrke, and Kristian Berg Harpviken, *Afghan Refugees in Iran: From Refugee Emergency to Migration Management*, Oslo: Chr. Michelsen Institute, June 2004.

"Taliban Confirms FNA Report on Recent Visit to Tehran," Fars News Agency, June 3, 2013. As of April 21, 2014:
http://english2.farsnews.com/newstext.php?nn=9202247052

Tang, Alisa, "Iran Forcibly Deports 100,000 Afghans," Associated Press, June 15, 2007. As of November 6, 2013:
http://www.washingtonpost.com/wp-dyn/content/article/2007/06/15/AR2007061500292_pf.html

"Tehran Battles Drugs, Addiction and Crime," *Al-Monitor*, March 15, 2013. As of April 21, 2014:
http://www.al-monitor.com/pulse/originals/2013/05/iran-drugs-heroin-crime-tehran.html.

Tennyson, K. N., "India-Iran Relations: Challenges Ahead," *Air Power*, Vol. 7, No. 2, 2012, pp. 153–171.

Tharoor, Ishaan, "Iran's Arrest of an Extremist Foe: Did Pakistan Help?" *Time*, February 25, 2010. As of November 7, 2013:
http://www.time.com/time/world/article/0,8599,1968126,00.html

Torabi, Yama, *The Growing Challenge of Corruption in Afghanistan: Reflections on a Survey of the Afghan People, Part 3 of 4*, Washington, D.C.: Asia Foundation, 2012.

Umid, N., "Iran Agrees to Barter Wheat from Pakistan," *Trend*, July 13, 2013. As of November 7, 2013:
http://en.trend.az/capital/business/2170715.html

United Nations Office on Drugs and Crime, *World Drug Report 2012*, Vienna: United Nations, 2012.

"U.S.-India Joint Statement," White House Office of the Press Secretary, September 27, 2013. As of November 7, 2013:
http://www.whitehouse.gov/the-press-office/2013/09/27/us-india-joint-statement

Vatanka, Alex, "The Guardian of Pakistan's Shia," *Current Trends in Islamist Ideology*, Vol. 13, 2012, pp. 5–17. As of November 7, 2013:
http://www.hudson.org/content/researchattachments/attachment/1144/201207271_currenttrendsvol13.pdf

———, "Problems in the Pipeline: Energy-Starved Pakistan Looks to Iran for Natural Gas," *The Majalla*, May 2, 2013. As of November 7, 2013:
http://www.majalla.com/eng/2013/05/article55241015

Weitz, Richard, "Russia's 'Return' to Afghanistan," *World Politics Review*, January 25, 2011. As of November 7, 2013:
http://www.worldpoliticsreview.com/articles/print/7653

World Bank, *Afghanistan in Transition: Looking Beyond 2014*, Vol. 1, Washington, D.C.: World Bank, May 2012. As of October 14, 2013:
http://siteresources.worldbank.org/AFGHANISTANEXTN/Images/305983-1334954629964/AFTransition2014Vol2.pdf

Wolf, Siegfried O., "Post-2014 Afghanistan: Future Scenarios from Structure and Agency Perspectives," *Journal of South Asian Development*, Vol. 8, No. 2, 2013, pp. 233–254.

The World Factbook, Afghanistan, CIA. As of October 14, 2013:
https://www.cia.gov/library/publications/the-world-factbook/geos/af.html

Zambelis, Chris, "Back with a Vengeance: The Baloch Insurgency in Iran," *Terrorism Monitor*, Vol. 9, No. 2, 2011. As of November 7, 2013:
http://www.jamestown.org/single/?no_cache=1&tx_ttnews%5Btt_news%5D=37365&tx_ttnews%5BbackPid%5D=515#.UgVuB5LVDX4

———, "The Day After: Iran's Quiet Taliban Diplomacy Reflects Preparations for a Post-U.S. Afghanistan," *Terrorism Monitor*, Vol. 11, No. 21, 2013, pp. 7–10.

Interviews with the Authors

Afghan analyst, January 4, 2013.

Afghan businessman, January 1, 2013.

Afghan media leader, February 23, 2013.

Afghan official, February 21, 2013, and February 26, 2013.

Afghan religious leader, January 1, 2013.

Afghan researcher, January 4, 2013.

Afghan scholar, January 2, 2013, and February 19, 2013.

Former Afghan official, January 2, 2013, February 20, 2013, and February 24, 2013.

Former senior Afghan government official, February 24, 2013.

Former senior Afghan official, January 1, 2013, February 20, 2013, and February 24, 2013.

Influential Afghan, February 19, 2013, February 23, 2013, and February 24, 2013.

Prominent Afghan businessman, January 4, 2013.

Prominent Afghan Shia leader, January 1, 2013.

Senior Afghan government official, February 26, 2013.

Senior Afghan official, February 21, 2013.

Senior Afghan security official, January 2, 2013, and February 19, 2013.